eSPORTS

THE ULTIMATE GAMER'S GUIDE

HARPER

An Imprint of HarperCollinsPublishers

CONTENTS

INTRODUCTION

Esports are the act of playing a video game competitively. For the most part the term esports has come to be associated with a certain group of video games, but in reality, any time you play a video game competitively (whether that be directly against another person or trying to beat a high score), that is an esport.

WHILE video games have been played competitively since the first games were created back in the 1960s, the esports industry has grown quickly in the last few years, and today is worth billions of dollars. The industry is still young and growing at a rapid pace, but already millions of dollars are given away as prize money and sponsorship deals can be worth many millions more.

In the current era, there are a few top games that people will mostly be referring to when they mention esports. First-person shooter *Counter-Strike: Global Offensive* and **MOBAs** such as *League of Legends* and *DotA 2* are currently the biggest esports in the world, but new competitive titles are released every week and many have a chance at dethroning these kings of the industry.

Esports events now sell out massive stadiums and bring in millions of viewers across the world. TV networks are fighting it out to get the broadcast rights to these events, while big name brands want to be the main sponsor to try to get their name out to the primarily young audience that esports brings in.

The best gamers are the celebrities of today, boasting millions of social media followers and very healthy bank accounts. Some of the top players are multimillionaires from prize winnings alone, not counting their base salary or any sponsorship deals they may have.

Despite all of this growth, the industry is still fairly young and one that a lot of people don't fully understand. Esports is about as far from the old gamer stereotypes as you can get. Instead of sitting inside staring at a TV, these players are packing arenas, often selling more tickets than football matches, bringing in millions of viewers, and making more money from one event than most will in a lifetime.

The rapidly changing landscape of esports, along with the wealth of information out there, can make it quite difficult to get into and understand what is going on, especially to those who haven't grown up with video games. However, esports is an incredibly welcoming community for the most part, and once you get up to speed on the basics, you're sure to love what you see.

This book is designed to guide you through the basics of the world of esports, detailing all of the top games, the big events, and more than a few of the names you should be looking out for. Once you've read through these pages, you should know more than enough to jump online and start watching esports events or even start playing in them yourself. Your entry to one of the fastest-growing industries in the world starts here …

THE HISTORY OF ESPORTS

Some people believe that Riot Games invented esports in 2009 with the release of *League of Legends*. Others believe that it started when online tournaments began in the late 1990s, after internet access became common for home gamers. However, the real answer lies further back in gaming history, although at the time they had no idea that what they were doing would become known as esports . . .

THE first ever recorded esports tournament was held way back in 1972 at Stanford University in California. The game that was being played was *Spacewar!*, and the prize was a year's subscription to *Rolling Stone* magazine. Bruce Baumgart won the five-man tournament and claimed his prize, not knowing that years later he would become known as the winner of what is often regarded as the first esports tournament. While there's a good chance that there were other video game tournaments before this, it's the Stanford *Spacewar!* event that's considered to be the first actual recorded tournament. Of course there would be many more to come, but this may be the origin of esports as we know it.

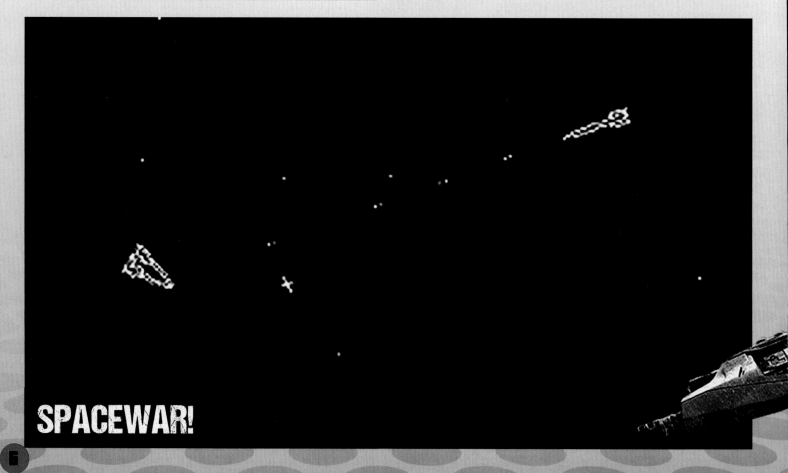

SPACEWAR!

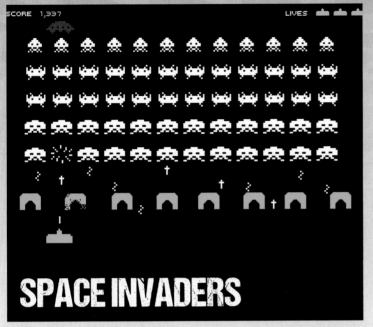

SPACE INVADERS

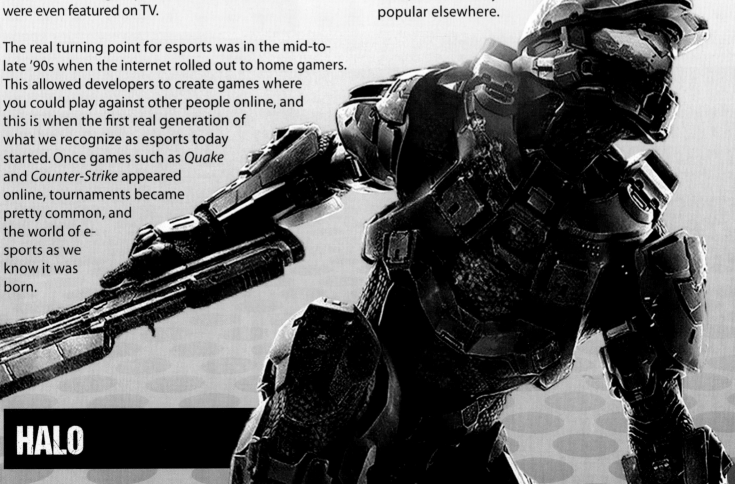

HALO

LAN parties also started to become a thing and some gamers would run tournaments, becoming the first real **LAN** competitions for this new breed of esports. They were a far cry from the events that sell out stadiums these days, and many of them had little to no prizes, but all great things have humble beginnings.

As this was happening in the West, South Korea decided it would roll out broadband internet all over the country. This, combined with the launch of the first *StarCraft* game, was one of the most important moments in esports history. Within a few years esports events were bringing in thousands of fans and could sell out stadiums. The popularity of *StarCraft* in Korea proved that esports could be more than a few people at a **LAN** party, and really got things going in the region.

Shortly after this, video game competitions would become pretty commonplace. As games started to pop up more and more, high scores became a hot competition, and tournaments were organized to see who could get the highest score. In 1980, the *Space Invaders* Championship welcomed over 10,000 participants, becoming the largest esports event ever at the time. Competitions like this would continue for many years, with some high score chasers becoming very well-known. Some events were even featured on TV.

As the internet became more common around the world, competition also became more common. By the mid-2000s, esports had started to become a big thing, with prize pools hitting tens of thousands of dollars in the West and Korea still going crazy for *StarCraft*. Games such as *Call of Duty* and *Halo* dominated in the US and UK, while *Counter-Strike* and mods, such as the original *DotA*, became very popular elsewhere.

The real turning point for esports was in the mid-to-late '90s when the internet rolled out to home gamers. This allowed developers to create games where you could play against other people online, and this is when the first real generation of what we recognize as esports today started. Once games such as *Quake* and *Counter-Strike* appeared online, tournaments became pretty common, and the world of e-sports as we know it was born.

THE HISTORY OF ESPORTS

Around the mid-2000s, a few big-name sponsors started to enter the **scene**. Intel started to work on the Intel Extreme Masters, which was a series of events that still run to this day. This is when money started to come into esports in the Western world, and slowly but surely everything started to grow.

By the late 2000s competition in video games was pretty standard. Organizations such as ESL and MLG were hosting tournaments in large venues with hundreds of thousands of dollars on the line, and communities for games were organizing their own major events. More and more sponsors were getting involved, and the new ability to show highlights on YouTube made things much more accessible.

However, arguably the most important thing to happen in the world of esports was the launch of **Twitch** in 2011. The streaming service designed for games made streaming live gameplay easy, or at least easier than it had ever been. It also provided a centralized source for all game streams, meaning you could go from watching *Call of Duty* to *StarCraft* without having to change websites.

Twitch made it easy to watch esports, and as a result this brought in a lot more viewers. Keeping up to date with things before was hard work, especially for newcomers, but now they could just come to **Twitch** and instantly watch competitions live.

Around this time *League of Legends* exploded, the first *DotA 2* International took place, and *Call of Duty* truly became a mainstream hit franchise. All of this, and many more factors, resulted in esports viewership growing rapidly, and this brought in more and more sponsors, and more sponsors means more money, which made things sustainable.

A few years on and we find ourselves in a position that would have been close to unthinkable fifteen years ago. Esports events have millions of dollars on the line, tens of millions of people tune in for the biggest matches of the year, and thousands of people work full-time in the esports industry. Companies such as Chipotle, Coca-Cola and even car manufacturer Audi are signing sponsorship deals in the world of esports, and it is considered one of the fastest-growing sectors in the world.

Esports had some pretty humble beginnings, but it has grown into one of the most exciting industries in the world. The stories that it creates often match many of those from traditional sports, and in many ways improve upon them. There is still a ways to go yet, but there is no reason why some esports competitions couldn't be considered to be on the same level as the NFL or the Premier League within a few years ... and even further into the future than that, who knows what is possible?

DOTA 2

LEAGUE OF LEGENDS

HOW TO BE A PRO PLAYER

Anyone who is interested in the world of esports has probably dreamed of being one of the many pro players who can earn millions. Much like in traditional sports, many of these pros are idolized and fans want to be able to follow in their footsteps—after all, who wouldn't want to get paid to play video games professionally?

UNFORTUNATELY it isn't quite as simple as just wanting to be a pro player. A lot of work goes into making it to the top, and it really isn't easy, with only a tiny percentage of people who try ever making it a full-time career.

The most obvious thing that you need to become a pro player is to be very good at a game. For some this comes naturally, but for most this will involve a lot of work and constant practice. The first part of the puzzle is to find a game that has a strong esports **scene** and is one that you enjoy playing. There's no point in playing a game that's just not fun, as you will be miserable having to play it all day, every day. Plus, enjoying what you do is a key part to being a top pro player, and just everyday life in general!

Practicing every day and keeping up with everything that's going on in the world of esports is key. While it does happen, it is very rare that someone who has little knowledge of the pro **scene** makes it onto a top team. You need to know when a team is looking for a player, and what kind of player they need.

Next up, you need to get noticed, and you can do this in a number of different ways. The most obvious is to climb whatever ranked ladder your chosen game has. Leaderboards are designed to show the very best players, and anyone who makes it to the top will instantly become known to those in the pro **scene**. Others have made it in through good networking, or by creating content that gave them a big fanbase, but neither is particularly reliable. Of course, you can also join an amateur team and try to take them to the top.

But playing the game is not the only factor in becoming a pro player. For any team-based game you need to be able to socialize well and interact with your team, as a poor team atmosphere will not lead to any tournament wins. You also need to be an attractive proposition to organizations—few organizations will want to sign a player who has a poor attitude or is rude, so being a good person is always a positive.

There are many other things you need to consider before you start your journey to becoming a pro player. You need to be healthy (as injuries will be a big turn-off for teams), you need to be able to handle the pressure of playing in front of thousands of people and you need to be able to market yourself and build a personal fanbase.

EVENTS YOU NEED TO WATCH

 LCS

The LCS is the main *League of Legends* competition in both North America and Europe. Each year there are two ten week **splits**, with playoffs happening at the end of each. Then, at the end of each gaming year, there is one final tournament to decide the third team that will make it to the World Championship.

During each split, teams play matches weekly. In Europe, broadcast days are on Thursdays, Fridays and Saturdays, with occasional extra Sunday broadcasts.

In the US, broadcasts are on Fridays, Saturdays and Sundays. A number of matches are played each day, meaning there is more than just one match to watch.

LCS is definitely worth watching, as it is some of the best *League of Legends* competition in the world, and tuning in every week will mean that you can keep up to date on all of the major storylines. The excellent broadcast teams and production along with the regular schedule make this one of the easier events to watch.

THE INTERNATIONAL

The International (TI) is the largest esports competition in the world, with a prize pool that was more than $23 million in 2017. The event only comes around once each year, typically taking place in August, but when it is happening it is a must-watch tournament.

With so much money on the line, the teams give it their all to make sure they place highly. The International almost always features the best *DotA* matches of the year. The action is always very hyped up, and the massive crowd at the Key Arena responds in electric fashion, creating one of the best atmospheres of any esports events.

As **Valve** makes millions from crowd-funding the prize pool for the event, they always make sure that the broadcasts are of the highest quality. New features such as AR effects and detailed analysis in **weatherman segments** are often revealed at TI. **Valve** also runs a newbie stream that is aimed at new viewers who might not understand all of the goings-on.

ELEAGUE

ELEAGUE runs a number of events, and they have already hosted *CS:GO*, *Overwatch* and *Street Fighter* competitions since they started broadcasting in 2016. Even if they host an event in a game you have never watched before, it is certainly worth tuning in. They cut their teeth in the world of *CS:GO*, and remain one of the best tournament organizers on the **scene**, but they have also proven that they can handle any game that they choose to showcase.

As ELEAGUE is owned and run by Turner Broadcasting, everything they do has the quality of a TV broadcast. The ELEAGUE Arena looks like a top-tier TV set, and the broadcast talent they bring in know how to handle themselves on live TV. If you are looking for a slick broadcast that also features some top-tier action, then you really can't go wrong with ELEAGUE.

$1000

FaRRi^ Format ^^ @ Long A [RADIO]: Flashbang Out!

LEAGUE OF LEGENDS

League of Legends is undoubtedly the biggest esport in the world right now, and can also claim to be the biggest game in the world in pretty much every metric. More than 100 million people play the game every month, and hundreds of thousands tune in every week to watch the top level competitive action from around the world.

LEAGUE *of Legends* first started life in 2005, when Brandon "Ryze" Beck and Marc "Tryndamere" Merrill teamed up with Steve "Guinsoo" Feak and Steve "Pendragon" Mescon (who both worked on the original *DotA* in *Warcraft III*), to create a brand-new standalone **MOBA** like the world had never seen before.

Beck and Merrill founded the game development company Riot Games in 2006, but it took another two years for *League of Legends* to be officially revealed in late 2008. *LoL* stayed in development for quite a while and finally went into its first closed beta in April 2009, before opening up to the public later that year.

A **grassroots scene** sprang up in the initial years, with little money or support from Riot, who were too busy focusing on the game itself. However, after a couple of years, that changed significantly. In 2011, the first official world championship was held at DreamHack Summer, with just under $100,000 in prize money. It was incredibly successful and one of the biggest esports events ever.

Primary Quest

Destroy an Enemy Turre

Secondary Quest

Purchase a Starting Iter

Slay 5 Enemy Minion

Spells
Manaless Champions

Laning
Lane Names

The next year Riot held another world championship, but things were still very third-party led. That continued until mid-2012, when Riot announced they'd run the *League of Legends* Championship Series. This competition ran in North America and Europe starting in early 2013, with the best teams in each region competing in a regular league format. Riot decided to do everything themselves, from broadcasting to tournament management and even finding a place to hold the event.

The LCS expanded quickly and became the premier esports league. Now, hundreds of thousands of fans tune in to the competition every week, and some players earn upward of $100,000 a year in salary alone. The LCS is a big money league, proven by the broadcast rights being sold to BAMTech, the tech arm of Major League Baseball, for $50 million a year.

In 2018 the NA LCS will become the first franchised league in top level *LoL*. Any team could submit a proposal to get in, but they had to be selected by Riot and cough up $10 million for the privilege. These teams are now in the LCS for life, with relegation being scrapped. Many think this is a great move, as it should bring a lot more stability to the competition and make big-name sponsors a lot more comfortable in investing some cash.

The end of every competitive year is topped off with the World Championships. Teams from every competitive region compete to be crowned the best in the world and take home a chunk of cash. Over the last year Riot has decided to adopt a crowd-funding system for the prize pool, so it is expected that in a few years *LoL* Worlds could compete with the *DotA* International in terms of cash prizes.

LEAGUE OF LEGENDS

THE MAJOR LEAGUES

EU LCS

The EU LCS is the top league in Europe and one run entirely by Riot Games themselves. Teams compete in two **splits** each year, each of which has a ten week regular season, with the top teams then heading to the playoffs to determine the overall winner. The EU LCS still features relegation and promotion.

 LCK

The LCK is the top competition in South Korea and the best *LoL* league in the world. LCK teams have won four out of six world championships and dominate all other regions in international competition. The league itself is one of the most competitive out there, and many believe that a mid-table LCK team could dominate in EU or NA.

LMS

The LMS is the fifth major league and features teams from Hong Kong, Macau, and Taiwan. Initially these teams competed in the GPL, but Taiwan dominated the region so the LMS was created to break things up a little and give other SEA regions a better chance in competition. In recent years LMS teams have become serious players on the international circuit.

NA LCS

The NA LCS is similar to the EU LCS in many ways. However, from 2018 there will be one key difference, as the NA LCS will become a franchised league. Ten teams will be permanent members of the league, with relegation going out the door. The buy-in for the league was $10 million, and even then Riot had to turn down a lot of interested organizations.

LPL

The LPL is the main league in China and is operated by Tencent, the company that owns Riot Games and distributed *LoL* in China. The league used a group system in 2017, with teams being split into two groups during the regular season. The LPL has had a mixed history. At times it was considered the second best league in the world, and at others it has struggled at international competitions.

Select target(s).

FAKER

Lee "Faker" Sang Hyeok is undoubtedly the best *League of Legends* player of all time! The twenty-one-year-old Korean **mid laner** won the world championship in 2013, 2015 and 2016, and won the Mid Season Invitational in 2016 and 2017, making him the most successful player on the international circuit ever.

For the last few years he has been the star player on SK Telecom T1, the team that has dominated the LCK and international competitions. While other players have come and gone, Faker has always been the star player and has often single-handedly won them a crucial game. His ability to dominate the mid lane is better than anyone else in the world.

This success has made him a legend of the game. He could retire tomorrow and chances are no one would ever be able to match his achievements in international competition. When you ask anyone who the best *LoL* player is they will surely say Faker, and chances are they always will.

DOTA Z

Eggus of Immortality (michaele)

BATRIDER

245 / 891   +5.4
214 / 650   +2.0

66   35+4   2   9   18   41
20   140   100   225

3   340   22+4

6   486/600   36+14

The original *Defense of the Ancient (DotA)* mod for *Warcraft III* is actually what started this whole **MOBA** genre, and it's one that seems to have taken over the esports landscape. It is, and always will be, one of the most important video games. The original *DotA* mod had a pretty thriving competitive **scene**, with major events and quite a few sponsored teams. It never hit the heights of the console shooters that were popular at the time, but there was a dedicated community that made sure the **scene** was always growing.

N 2009 **Valve** announced that they had hired the mysterious Icefrog, who was one of the lead developers on the *Warcraft III DotA* mod. His mission was to create a standalone sequel to the mod, with the team at **Valve**. A year later, *DotA 2* was officially revealed in late 2010. Then in 2011 **Valve** announced that they would be holding the first ever *DotA 2* tournament, known as The International (TI), at Gamescom that year. The tournament was the first in esports history to give the winners $1,000,000, and was the first time we got to see the top *DotA* pros play on the game.

Shortly after, more and more players started to be invited to the closed beta of the game, with it eventually becoming open to everyone. Millions of players flooded to the game, and things really started to take off around TI 3 in 2013.

Obviously it was The International in 2011 that kick-started the competitive *DotA 2* **scene**, and the success of that tournament of course brought in other tournament organizers. In the first few years all of the big event organizers got involved, and while prize pools remained tiny compared to that of The International, the **scene** started to grow rapidly. It got to the stage where some teams were playing in multiple large events each month, making it one of the biggest and most popular esports in the world in early 2010s.

Valve continued to run TI each year, but outside of that they took a very hands-off approach in the early years. This allowed organizers such as ESL, DreamHack and StarLadder to run multiple events each year and reap the rewards. The **scene** continued to grow, but many worried that a lack of support from **Valve** and the increasing size of TI would have a negative impact.

Valve were reluctant to do more at first, but eventually decided to step in and take a little more control. They announced the Majors, a series of smaller events sponsored by **Valve** that would break the season up a little more, while they would still host TI every year.

This system certainly helped, and *DotA* is still at the top of the esports world (along with *LoL* and *CS:GO*), but it seems to be losing a little ground. *DotA* is close to going downhill, so hopefully **Valve**'s new proposition for third-party (see page 21) major events will help the **scene** retain its position at the top.

VALVE EVENTS

After kicking off the *DotA 2* competitive world in 2011, **Valve** took The International to Seattle for its second iteration and once again put up a $1.6 million prize pool for teams to compete for. But it was TI 3 that really got the **scene** to kick up a notch. For the first time **Valve** implemented crowd-funding to the prize pool. Fans could buy an in-game item, and 25 percent of each sale would be added to the prize pool. This resulted in the TI 3 prize pool totaling $2,874,380, becoming the biggest esports prize pool at the time.

Having made millions of dollars and helped out the pro scene at the same time, **Valve** unsurprisingly did the same thing for every International after that. TI 4 boasted a $10 million prize pool and TI 5 hit $18 million. But this created a problem: top teams started to play fewer events as it wasn't worth their time when they could be practicing for The International, which would set them up for life if they won. **Valve** realized this and eventually started to host the Majors.

In the 2015/16 season, **Valve** implemented the Majors, three tournaments set up and run by themselves. These events featured $3 million prize pools, which were still way bigger than any other third-party event, and split up the season. This also resulted in the creation of official transfer windows for players to move teams. TI was still held every year, with TI 6 being the first to break the $20 million mark, and TI 7 going over $24 million.

For the most part the Majors were a success and returned for the following season, albeit with one less tournament. They kept interest going all year long and brought some much-needed stability to the **scene**.

THE NEW-LOOK DOTA SCENE

Despite the success of the Majors, the *DotA* **scene** has remained pretty stagnant in terms of numbers. So, for the 17/18 season **Valve** made a change. No longer will they run any other tournaments outside of The International, but they will now work with third parties to run major and minor events. To become a major an event must have at least $500,000 up for grabs, with **Valve** adding another $500,000 to make $1,000,000. For minors the prize pool must be at least $150,000, with **Valve** adding another $150,000 to it.

These events will run throughout the year, and will award successful teams points. The number of points depends on the prize pool and the timing of the competition, but all majors and minors will hand them out. At the end of the season the teams with the most points from the entire year will be invited to The International. It is hoped that this change will make sure that the top teams play in as many events as possible to secure their spot at TI, and will make the **scene** more active than ever.

If this works out then there is no reason why *DotA* can't stay at the top of the esports world for a good few years to come!

THE DOTA MAJOR CHAMPIONSHIPS
FOUR ANNUAL TOURNAMENTS

FALL WINTER SPRING SUMMER

During the **Valve** Major era, there were two players who straight up dominated the **scene**. Between the 15/16 seasons and the 16/17 season, **Valve** hosted five Majors. OG won four of them. The only two players to stay on the team for all four wins were Tal "Fly" Aizik and Johan "N0tail" Sundstein. These four wins cemented them as two of the best *DotA* players ever!

COUNTER-STRIKE: GLOBAL OFFENSIVE

Counter-Strike (CS) has long been played competitively. As soon as online gaming became common in the early 2000s, *Counter-Strike* tournaments started to pop up all over the world. On the 1.6 version of the original *Counter-Strike* these tournaments grew to be pretty big, with international **LAN** events taking place multiple times a year. As early as 2001 these events were breaking the $100,000 prize pool mark, making *CS* one of the biggest esports in the world.

COUNTER-STRIKE 1.6 continued to be popular well into the late 2000s. In 2004, **Valve** released *Counter-Strike: Source*, a remake of the game on the new Source engine. Some players loved it, while others stuck with 1.6, creating a bit of a fractured **scene**. Competitions in both games continued to run, and both were very successful. In 2007 and 2008, Source was a big part of the Championship Gaming Series, a televised competition that featured some big money, but outside of these events it never quite hit the popularity of the original 1.6.

In 2012, **Valve** released *Counter-Strike: Global Offensive* (*CS:GO*). It was hoped that this would be the game that would bring together the fractured communities of 1.6 and *Source*, and become a major success in the esports world. While we know today that is exactly what happened, in the first few years it didn't look too likely. When the game was released many players stuck to their respective games, claiming that *CS:GO* had a lot of issues.

Over time more and more players started to move over to the new title, and it started to pick up some steam. However, the real boost to the game came in August 2013, when **Valve** released the Arms Deal update. This patch added alternate paint jobs for weapons, known as skins, which could be purchased and sold. This brought in a lot of new players, and the **scene** exploded.

The interest in the game meant that almost all 1.6 and *Source* competition dropped within a few months, and the big tournaments and teams all switched to *CS:GO*. The **scene** grew at a rapid rate, quicker than almost any **scene** before, and soon tournaments were hitting the $100,000 mark on a regular basis.

After staying away from the pro **scene** for a while, **Valve** eventually stepped in in late 2013, hosting the first Major in partnership with DreamHack. **Valve** supported the tournament and boosted the prize pool to $250,000, making it the world championship. The Major was a success, and **Valve** continued to work with organizers to host these $250,000 events three times a year.

Then, in 2016, **Valve** decided to change things a little. They upped the prize pool to a million dollars, but cut down to two Majors a year. This again brought in more and more viewers, with the ELEAGUE Major in early 2017 being the first esports event to break one million viewers on a single **Twitch** stream.

The Majors created so much interest in *CS:GO* and, along with the new character skins, turned the game into one of the biggest in the world. The popularity of it even got the likes of Turner Broadcasting to run *CS:GO* competitions in the form of ELEAGUE. These massive events combined with the Majors mean that *CS:GO* is one of the three biggest esports in the world right now, and shows no sign of slowing down.

PLAYING ON TEAM COUNTER-TERRORIST

BOT Neil $1000   BOT Walt $1000   BOT Graham $1000

$1000

TheSilviu is joining the Counter-Terrorist force

P2000

23

THE CS:GO DYNASTIES

NINJAS IN PYJAMAS (NIP)

In the early days of *CS:GO*, NiP were unstoppable. They had some ridiculous win streaks and won almost every **LAN** they attended. The team of Christopher "GeT_RiGhT" Alesund, Patrik "f0rest" Lindberg, Richard "Xizt" Lanström, Adam "friberg" Friberg and Robin "Fifflaren" Johansson proved to be near unstoppable, and they were the biggest names in the **scene** for the first few years. They made it to the final of the first three Majors, but only managed to win on their third attempt. Recent years have not been kind, and multiple roster changes have followed, but NiP remain one of the most popular teams in the world, thanks to their early dominance.

Fnatic was the team that won the first Major way back in 2013, but it wasn't until 2014 that the team became undoubtedly the best in the world. While the roster that won DreamHack Winter 2013 did well, it wasn't enough to keep them together. By mid-2014 the Fnatic roster consisted of Robin "flusha" Rönnquist, Jesper "JW" Wecksell, Markus "pronax" Wallsten, Olof "olofmeister" Kaibier Gustafsson and Freddy "KRiMZ" Johansson. This roster would go on to win almost every competition they entered in late 2014 and early 2015, before taking both ESL One Katowice and ESL One Cologne, both of which were Majors. In recent years a series of lineup changes has left Fnatic struggling a little at major events.

FNATIC

SK Gaming, or Luminosity as they were first known, became the best team in the world in 2016. At the MLG Columbus Major they were expected to do well, but few had them down as winning. But that is exactly what they did and took first place at the first million dollar Major. After this they continued to win events and transferred to SK Gaming. They then ended up winning ESL One Cologne, the second Major of the year, to establish themselves as one of the great teams. The lineup from 2016 featured Gabriel "FalleN" Toledo, Fernando "fer" Alvarenga, Marcelo "coldzera" David, Lincoln "fnx" Lau and Epitácio "TACO" do Melo. fnx ended up leaving the team, being replaced by João "felps" Vasconcellos, but this didn't impact the team's performance too much, and they are still one of the best teams in the world.

SK GAMING

VIRTUS.PRO

While the other teams have enjoyed one lengthy run at the top, Virtus.Pro have always been up there, bar a couple of very notable poor runs. The team has been together pretty much since day one. They officially joined forces in 2013, when *CS:GO* was very much in its early days, and have dominated the **scene** since. They only won one Major, back in 2014, but have been a top-four team ever since. They won the first season of ELEAGUE, came second at the ELEAGUE Major and have a ton of other **LAN** wins. Mid-2016 was perhaps their worst run ever, crashing out of both major online leagues, but they still managed to make the top four at the Krakow Major. The team of Wiktor "TaZ" Woitas, Filip "NEO" Kubski, Jaroslaw "pashaBiceps" Jarzabkowski, Janusz "Snax" Pogorzelski and Pawel "byali" Bielinski will forever be legends of the game.

HEROES OF THE STORM

Considering that the **MOBA** genre was created in *Warcraft III* (a Blizzard game), the company was pretty slow to release its own version. Blizzard *DotA*, as it was first known, was in development for some time, but it didn't launch until 2015, when it was known as *Heroes of the Storm*.

BY this time *DotA* and *League of Legends* were already massive, and were the two biggest esports in the world. *Smite* was comfortably in the number three position, and many questioned if there was a space for Blizzard's title. It found an audience, as all Blizzard games do, but it never quite hit the heights of the other two major **MOBAs**, or that of other Blizzard games. Blizzard has a reputation for defining or creating a genre with each of its titles, but *HotS* was the one that failed to do that in many people's eyes.

Fortunately the audience that it did find was very keen on getting a pro **scene** going. There were competitions being held during the alpha and beta tests, and while things were still quite small a **scene** did emerge in the early days. It grew after launch, and large organizers such as ESL and DreamHack started to get involved.

Things grew to be pretty big at the end of the first year, with many third-party tournaments breaking the $100,000 mark, but after the initial good start things started to turn sour quickly. Top organizations began

to drop their rosters, and some of the best players in the world considered trying to switch to other esports games because of a lack of consistent money. The **scene** didn't crash, but it was close to it.

HEROES OF THE STORM

HGC

Fortunately Blizzard decided they wanted to control all their esports competitions right around the time when *Heroes of the Storm* (*HotS*) was starting to struggle, and they came in and took over the *HotS* **scene**. Blizzard introduced the *Heroes of the Storm Global Championship* for the 2016 season; although it was a step in the right direction, it still wasn't quite enough.

In the first year, they organized regional competitions that would see teams fight on **LAN** for $100,000 multiple times a year. This was great, but prize money was still limited outside these events and cross-region play was very limited. Things improved for sure, but teams were still dropping rosters.

For 2017 they overhauled the whole thing. This started off with online regional leagues, which featured regular matches with good-quality broadcasts. The NA, Korean, and EU versions of these featured massive $425,000 prize pools. Following these the top teams would qualify for the Western or Eastern Clash, a **LAN** event bringing multiple regions together.

Then, at the end of each phase, of which there were two, the top teams would head to a fully international competition. These tournaments had very large prize pools and would determine who the best team in the world actually was.

This format for the HGC worked better, and introduced regular international play for the first real time. Prize money went up, and everyone seems to be happy with the results. *HotS* will likely never topple *DotA* or *LoL*, but right now it has that third spot on lockdown.

LORE OF THE LAND

One of the advantages that *Heroes of the Storm* has over both *League of Legends* and *DotA 2* is that Blizzard has a wealth of characters to draw from. This is one of the reasons why *HotS* did so well in the early days, as people wanted to see how a character from *StarCraft* would interact with someone from the *Diablo* universe. Every one of the characters in the game had featured in another Blizzard game in one way or another, and this made Blizzard fans very excited.

When *HotS* launched it was full of characters from the *StarCraft*, *Diablo* and of course *Warcraft* universes, but further characters have added the world of *Overwatch*, and even some more niche Blizzard titles such as *The Lost Vikings*. All of these universes meet on the battlefields of *HotS*, creating a somewhat dreamlike situation for hardcore Blizzard fans.

Impressively Blizzard even managed to find a way of justifying this whole thing with some pretty deep lore. While we all know that the various characters could never meet in their respective universes, the Nexus can bring them all together. The Nexus is a transdimensional storm and a strange limbo of clashing universes. Fortunately all of those universes are Blizzard-owned ones, and can bring heroes together onto the battlefields. The Nexus also means that all hero deaths are temporary in this new realm, giving a bit of lore as to why heroes can respawn.

It is impressive that Blizzard went to this length to make sure that the lore of *HotS* actually explained why all these heroes were meeting for the first time. They could have just ignored it, but instead they gave the superfans some reasoning for the crazy meetings that go on.

FNATIC'S 2017 DOMINANCE

In the pro **scene**, 2017 was dominated by one team. Fnatic have proved time and time again that they are perhaps the best team in the world right now and show no sign of stopping anytime soon. In the first seven months of the year, Fnatic placed in the top two of all competitions they entered, and they ended up winning the massive Mid Season Brawl that saw teams from across the world compete. This earned them a cool $100,000 and sent a message to the rest of the world. Their long-term rivals Team Dignitas have fallen off a little, so as of 2017 Fnatic can be classed as the best team in the world!

STARCRAFT II

As with *DotA 2*, *StarCraft* is credited as one of the games that started esports. While video game tournaments were around since the first titles started to emerge, these were small-scale local affairs. However, *StarCraft* became a phenomenon. Massive international events were held, thousands of dollars were put up as prizes, and in one nation it became a cultural icon.

THE first *StarCraft* launched in 1998 and became a worldwide success. However, in South Korea it became much more than that. *StarCraft*, and its *Brood War* expansion, became the national sport of South Korea in the early 2000s. Everyone in the country knew what it was, and this was the first time that competitive video games really took off in a massive way.

Brood War enjoyed success across the world, but South Korea was its home. The esports industry became a thing and everyone wanted a piece of it. Matches were televised, major brands came in as sponsors, and the best players became celebrities. It really was unheard of for this kind of thing to happen, and it's safe to say that *StarCraft* was by far the biggest esport in the world for a number of years.

But in 2010, Blizzard released *StarCraft II*, the sequel to the much-loved game, and everything changed. A bigger audience was brought in worldwide and the global *StarCraft* **scene** started to grow. Korea was pretty slow in adopting the new title fully, mostly because of some serious IP rights conflicts in the region, but within a couple of years it was the title that was played in all the major leagues. This was a new era for *StarCraft*.

The core gameplay remained pretty much the same—this was still an RTS that required a lot of quick reactions and strategic decision-making, but everything was improved. The success of *Brood War* also meant that *StarCraft II* launched with a ton of esports features, such as a proper **spectator mode**, something that no one imagined the first game would ever need when making it.

StarCraft II took its place at the top of the esports scene, but never hit the heights of *Brood War* in Korea. *League of Legends* started to challenge *StarCraft* for the top spot, but for a while *StarCraft* held strong. Tournaments grew a lot in the early days and all was good. But then after a few years, the landscape changed. *StarCraft's* viewing numbers in the West started to drop, with the **MOBAs** and *CS:GO* growing rapidly. In Korea some started to return to *Brood War,* and by 2014 some big organizers in Korea brought back *Brood War* competitions.

The **scene** started to shrink, and, while new expansions helped a bit, it was clear that *StarCraft* just didn't have the same popularity level as the new breed of esports. It certainly didn't die, especially in Korea, but it did drop to the second tier of esports where it still sits today.

These days, outside of Korea, the audience is a lot smaller than it once was. However, it still remains one of the most important esports of all time and should be remembered forever.

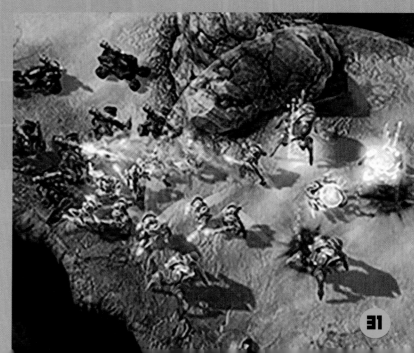

KOREA'S GAME

In Korea, both *Brood War* and *StarCraft II* became cultural sensations. *Brood War* was selling out stadiums in the country before Riot Games even existed, and hundreds of thousands would watch matches on national TV. It's difficult to explain just how big *StarCraft* is in Korea, but comparisons to the Premier League and NFL aren't too far off!

This popularity of course meant that almost all the best players in the world came from Korea. Outside of a few notable examples, almost every top-tier player in both titles has been Korean. These big-name players became so popular in the country that they were treated as celebrities.

Names such as Lee "Flash" Young Ho and Lee "Jaedong" Jae Dong became as recognizable in South Korea as pro football players are in the US, and even on the worldwide stage they became legends within the community.

Even when the **scene** was rocked by major controversies, such as serious game-fixing issues, some of which even resulted in suspended jail sentences for former pros, the hardcore Korean fanbase did not turn away.

LEE "JAEDONG" JAE DONG

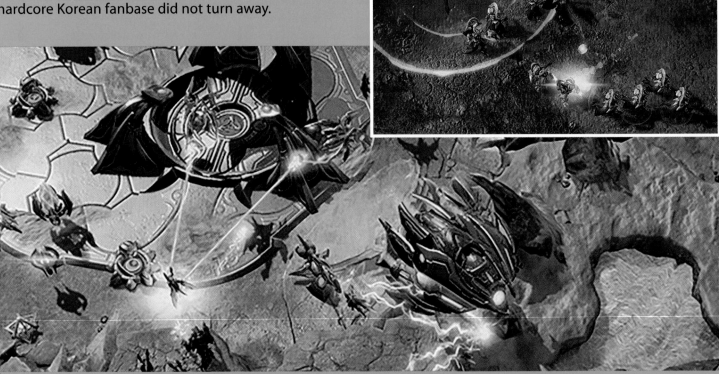

BROOD WAR REMASTERED

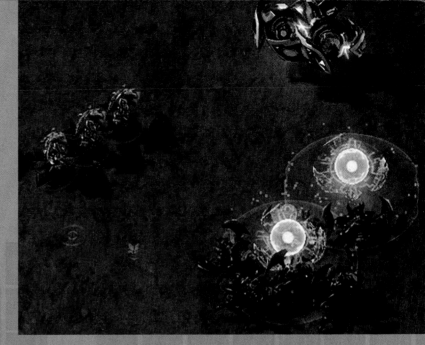

In August of 2017, Blizzard released *StarCraft Remastered*, an updated version of the original *StarCraft* and its *Brood War* expansion. With *StarCraft II* struggling and the appetite for *Brood War* returning to Korea, Blizzard decided to remaster the game that started this whole thing off, and updated it in all the right areas.

The core gameplay was kept exactly the same, so much so that there was cross play between the original version, which was updated with some new tweaks and made free, and the new remastered version. The single-player campaign was also left intact, with the only gameplay changes being cosmetic, with 4K visuals and updated audio.

The important features that were added included proper matchmaking, which made sure you could be matched against someone with a similar skill level, **Battle.net** integration, and **cloud saving**. All of these quality-of-life changes meant the game was much more player-friendly, while not compromizing on the classic gameplay at all.

Early signs are good for this remastering, with the Korean launch event bringing in thousands of viewers in person. It would be a surprise if *StarCraft Remastered* became as big as the original *Brood War*, but it is certainly a strong possibility.

WHERE TO WATCH

TWITCH

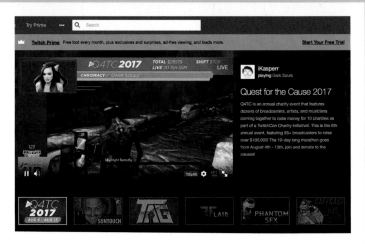

Twitch is the main platform for watching esports. The online streaming site was basically created for esports gaming and features broadcasts of almost every large event imaginable. If you know an event you want to watch is going to be on, then the first place to check is **Twitch**, as chances are it will be broadcast on there in some form. Competitions such as the LCS, *DotA 2* International, *CS:GO* Majors and many, many more are all streamed on **Twitch**.

The site also allows anyone to stream, so if there isn't a tournament going on at a particular time of the year, you can guarantee that there will be more than a few big name players streaming their practice games, or just having some fun.

Twitch is also available on almost every gaming platform under the sun, meaning you don't have to be sitting at a PC to watch. The PlayStation 4 and Xbox One both have **Twitch** apps, while mobile apps for iOS and Android will allow you to stream to any connected TV you may have.

YOUTUBE

While YouTube was a little slow to embrace esports, it now features streams for a lot of big-name events. Most large competitions, such as the LCS or *DotA 2* International, will stream on both YouTube and **Twitch**, so you can choose your preferred service. In general, more events seem to favor **Twitch** over YouTube.

However, YouTube has signed some big exclusivity deals with esports events, which means the competition is only streamed on YouTube. Both the ESL Pro League and ESC *CS:GO* leagues are now exclusive to YouTube.

IN-GAME

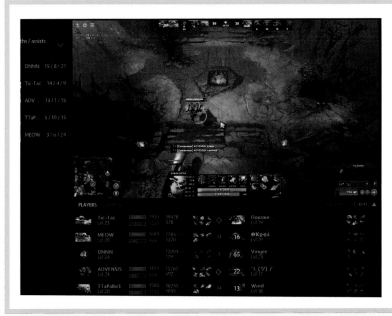

Some titles allow you to watch the top-level matches in the game itself. Arguably the best example of this is *DotA 2*, which allows anyone to watch any match being played in a public lobby. For tournaments, it is possible to watch the match in-game with full commentary from the **casters** and even the observer feed. However, if you wish, you can control the camera yourself.

Other titles such as *CS:GO* also offer very similar functionality, while some titles simply include an embed of the stream on the main menu, or create the option to watch the stream from the game itself.

TV

In recent years more and more events have been broadcast on TV. In the US, TBS features all ELEAGUE competitions, while in the UK the BBC and BT Sports picked up broadcast rights for the Gfinity Elite Series.

CASTERS AND VOICES

Whenever you watch any kind of esport, you can guarantee there will be someone casting it. While the in-game action itself is usually very entertaining, having a commentator or two (or even three in some cases) to walk you through the action adds an extra level of depth to the broadcast. While it seems like it is the easiest job in the world (after all, they are just talking over a video game,) there is actually a lot of skill involved in casting.

THE job of the **caster** is to keep the audience informed of what is happening, and also to control the pace of the broadcast. They need to choose when to get hyped up, when to show that something big or important is happening, and when to bring the pace down to give everyone a break. If esports were action and hype all the time, they would be very difficult to watch. But if the broadcast is very slow and dry, then everyone may get bored within a minute or two and go watch something else.

Different **casters** have different styles, but for the most part you can expect the broadcast team to have at least one play-by-play **caster**, who calls out the action when it kicks off, guiding the viewer through what is happening

and pointing out the big plays. They will be joined by a color **caster**, who provides an analytical look at the goings-on in the game during any downtime. They will explain why a player did what they did, and why that was a big deal, instead of just calling out what is going on.

A good casting duo can make or break a broadcast. Strong **casters** can bring the entertainment factor to even the most tedious of matches. Esports is full of top-quality competitions that are all-out action, but sometimes a match just doesn't deliver on its entertainment value. Here it is down to the **casters** to create some kind of extra entertainment, either through humor, extra-detailed insight into what went wrong, or just simply trying to create some kind of storyline around the match that interests the viewers.

OTHER BROADCAST ROLES

While the **casters** are the ones who will be bringing you the action when the game is on, there are also a lot of other people you can expect to see on the broadcast team.

The event host will usually lead a group of analysts to break down matches after they have finished and then set up the storylines for the next match during the downtime between games.

There may also be a stage host, who will introduce the teams onstage, get the crowd hyped, and conduct interviews with the players. Some events will also have a dedicated interviewer who will speak to the players backstage.

Of course, there are a lot of other roles that may pop up. Some members of the team create video content to keep viewers entertained during the breaks, some will be there to translate interviews, and some will be there to control the camera in-game.

GET INVOLVED ONLINE

While a lot of the elite-level competition in every esport happens at **LAN** events, almost anyone can sign up and play in competitions online. Regardless of the video game you want to play, there will almost always be some way of finding ways to play competitive games online, and you can sometimes even earn good money while doing so.

OPEN QUALIFIERS

Many of the biggest **LAN** events will feature open qualifiers. These online competitions allow anyone to sign up and compete to win a spot at the **LAN**. Usually these open qualifiers won't offer up any kind of prize money, but a win will get you a spot at the event, which often has quite a bit of cash up for grabs.

Most games have open qualifiers for large events, and they aren't as popular as you might think. While thousands of teams sign up to try and make it to The International, a lot fewer try out for smaller **LAN** events. Chances are, unless you turn out to be a superstar in the making, you won't make it to the **LAN**, but the qualifiers are your best chance at playing against a pro team.

FACEIT, GAMEBATTLES AND ESEA

Many companies, including but not limited to FACEIT, ESEA, and MLG, with its GameBattles system, allow you to simply go online, find some teammates, and then play in a competitive-style match. Of course playing with random people every time isn't quite the same as playing in a structured competition, but it is very close and you can do this whenever. Some of these **pickup group leagues** even offer cash rewards for those who do well during a season. For the most part you will be matched with players of a similar skill set, so this is the way to go if you want to play competitive style matches, but know you aren't quite good enough to go pro.

LOWER-TIER LEAGUES

While most people care about the big name competitions with thousands, or even millions of dollars on the line, there are a lot of lower-level competitions that you can try out. These amateur leagues vary from game to game, but they allow less-skilled players to compete for some cash in a setting where they actually have a chance to win. If you can find a group of like-minded players to join you in these competitions that have a regular schedule and are sometimes even casted and streamed matches, then you could win some cash and start to climb up the rankings.

IN-GAME COMPETITIONS

Some esports titles offer competition directly within the game, outside of the normal matchmaking. Titles such as *Call of Duty* have game modes that follow the event ruleset exactly, but match you with random players. Others, such as *DotA 2*, feature weekly in-game events where four friends are matched up against other teams in a small-scale bracket.

OVERWATCH

Overwatch was probably the first top-tier esport title to launch with the intention of actually being a dedicated esport game, following the early boom in 2010. After emerging from the ashes of Blizzard's *Titan* project (which at one point was rumored to be a *WoW* successor), *Overwatch* launched in 2016 and soon established the hero shooter genre, which is now more popular than ever.

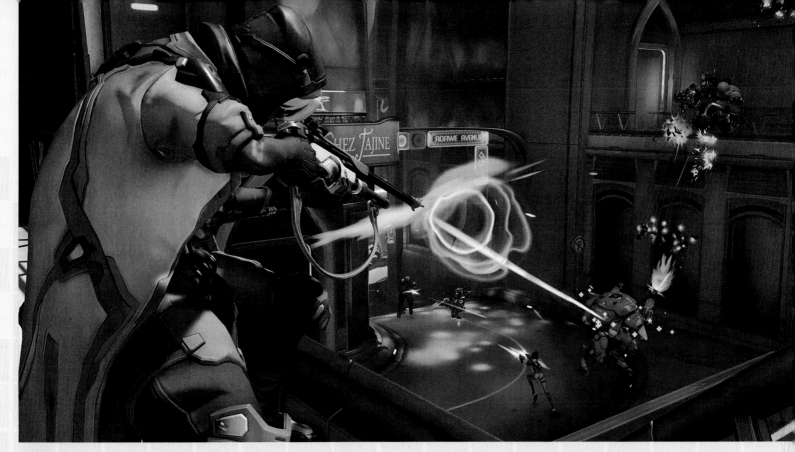

HE game itself combines elements of typical first-person shooters with the hero and ability systems of a **MOBA**, to create a fast-paced but incredibly strategic shooter. Each of the characters in *Overwatch* is very different and has unique abilities that will make them good in some situations and poor in others. Teams of six battle it out across a number of maps, some of which require both teams to try and capture a single location and hold it. Others have one team trying to push a payload from one end to the other, while the rival team tries to stall their progress until the time runs out.

When the title launched in 2016 it instantly became a hit, selling millions of copies. As of 2017 more than 30 million people have played *Overwatch* around the world, making it one of the most successful first years for a game ever. This resulted in a competitive **scene** being formed before the game had even officially launched, where major organizations had signed teams, and tournaments were taking place in the beta.

In the months after launch the **scene** exploded, with regular **LAN** events and rapidly growing prize pools. Events such as the Atlantic Showdown and the *Overwatch* Open offered up prize pools of hundreds of thousands of dollars just months after launch. In contrast it took *CS:GO* years to hit that kind of money. Blizzard even organized a World Cup, where players competed in national sides, as a show tournament for Blizzcon.

Then at Blizzcon, the *Overwatch* League was announced—a franchised worldwide **LAN** competition that would see each team hold a city. In time, Blizzard wanted matches to be played home and away, with teams traveling the world for each game that they played. While this sounded great at the time, it actually had a negative effect in the short term.

A high buy-in price for the league and uncertainty around revenue shares and value meant that a lot of big organizations dropped their teams. At the same time third-party tournament organizers such as ESL and FACEIT stopped organizing major *Overwatch* events, as in just a few months Blizzard would take over everything and leave them with no slice of the pie. This meant that 2017 was rough for pro *Overwatch*, but things are starting to look up with the *Overwatch* league kicking off.

OVERWATCH

The initial *Overwatch* League reveal will probably be looked back on as one of the biggest and most significant announcements in the history of esports. This was the first time in the modern era where a developer came in and said they would be doing everything and making an extremely exclusive league. They had a plan, and for the most part they executed it how they envisioned it.

While the league is still in its infancy, it's clear the *Overwatch* League is quickly becoming a premium brand. When people like Robert Kraft (who owns the New England Patriots) buy spots in the league, then you know that Blizzard has put forward quite a detailed plan, especially when it is believed Kraft and other owners put down $20 million to join.

Give the league a year or two and it could quite easily be the biggest out there, even taking over Riot's LCS for the top spot. The mainstream interest has been high, even in the early days, and everyone seems to want to be involved. All Blizzard has to do now is carry that strong momentum and mainstream interest through the first couple of seasons and they could be onto a real winner!

It's unlikely that the *Overwatch* League will beat the numbers put up by the likes of the Premier League or the NFL, but at this stage it does seem like the esports league with the highest potential to get close. It will be a very interesting few years to see how this develops …

BE A TEAM PLAYER

When playing *Overwatch* at a high level, even if it's just with a bunch of random players in competitive matchmaking, making sure that you have a solid team composition is absolutely essential. If you refuse to budge on your set hero and end up with six damage dealers, then chances are you are going to lose that match, and will probably get quite frustrated in the process.

Fortunately the heroes in *Overwatch* are split up into different categories…

ATTACK

Attack characters will do a lot of damage, although they tend to have weaker defenses.

DEFENSE

Defense characters have traits that are good at stopping opponents in their tracks.

TANKS

Tanks can absorb damage, distracting enemies from the rest of your team.

SUPPORTS

Supports are the ones who can offer heals or shields to teammates and generally keep them alive.

Now, it doesn't take a genius to work out that you are going to need a solid mix of each category to make your team work.

For the most part, attack and defense heroes are pretty interchangeable, but outside of that it is vital that you have a good mix of each group. Having at least one tank means they can draw fire from the heroes who can do some real damage, essentially becoming one big distraction. Winston, the gorilla scientist from the Moon, is perfect for this as he can leap around and make sure that everyone follows him, and not the characters with less health. While enemies are distracted by him, your damage dealers can then stand back and safely shoot from a distance.

However, the really important class to have is supports, and it seems like no one likes to play them. Jump into a public game and you can be sure that shouts of "We need a healer" will be thrown out every other second, but no one is willing to give up their precious Hanzo to make sure that the team has the ability to heal. Of course everyone wants to be the star of the show, getting all the kills and that awesome play-of-the-game that will set YouTube alight, but without a solid supporting cast that will almost never happen.

The moral here is that you need to be flexible if you want to win. If you get a team of stubborn players who won't change hero, then maybe it falls to you to pick up the baton and take a Lucio or Mercy into battle. Who knows, you might even enjoy it!

CALL OF DUTY

The most successful console franchise of recent times has been a top esport for years. While it has never quite hit the heights of *League of Legends* or *CS:GO*, *Call of Duty* has a very loyal fanbase that will watch everything. This leads to many events having very high viewing figures, compared to games of a similar size.

WHILE the *Call of Duty* games have been played competitively since 2003, it wasn't until the fourth iteration, *Call of Duty 4: Modern Warfare (CoD 4)*, that it really took off in the world of esports. *CoD 4* was one of the largest competitive games in the mid-to-late 2000s, and its impact is still felt in the industry to this day. Many of the top broadcast talents got their start in the world of *CoD*, either as a player or a broadcaster.

As the franchise continued to release games annually, the esports **scene** generally moved on to the next game. With the exception of *World at War*, almost every title released became the competitive game of

CWL

After years of hosting a world championship but very little else, Activision decided they were going to go for more of a Riot Games model and control all of their esports activities themselves. Alongside the release of *Black Ops 3* in 2015 came the *Call of Duty* World League, or CWL for short. The first year of the CWL involved two online stages where teams would play matches weekly in their own regions. At the end of each stage each region would have a play-off **LAN** event to decide the winners. Dotted alongside this online season were a few one-off **LAN** events, and at the end of the year was the annual World Championship.

This initial format proved controversial. There was no doubting that regulated competition that lasted the

choice. In 2011 publisher Activision got involved with the esports **scene** in a big way by hosting a $1,000,000 event called *CoD* XP. The event was a celebration of all things *CoD*, but the main focus for many was on the competition. The success of this event resulted in Activision hosting an annual world championship, *CoD* Champs, before taking complete control of the **scene** with the CWL in the 15/16 season.

Traditionally North America has dominanted since the event began, but recently the UK and Ireland have challenged the big US teams. Splyce became the first non-NA team to win a Major event in the CWL when they took home the Stage One Championship in 2016.

entire year was a good thing, but the lack of interregion play and the sparse **LAN** events drew criticism. As a result the league was completely overhauled when *Infinite Warfare* launched in 2016.

The *Infinite Warfare* esports season started out with a number of **LAN** events across the globe. Some were region-specific, and some were open to all comers. While the prize money is always a main focus, players competed in these events to get pro points. The higher you finished, the more points you got. Players could also earn limited points by playing online matches called GameBattles, and in weekly online competitions. Midway through the season the top teams from each region were invited to the CWL Global Pro League, a **LAN** competition that would see four groups of four teams battle it out at the MLG studios. A second season of the GPL took place shortly after and then, as ever, *CoD* Champs returned to end the season.

CALL OF DUTY
WORLD LEAGUE
ESPORTS

INFINITE WARFARE

Infinite Warfare was released in November 2016 and was the lead title for *Call of Duty* esports throughout the following twelve months. It was the third game in the series to feature the advanced-movement systems that allowed players to fly around the game with jetpack-like suits. The futuristic setting saw the game head to space for the first time, although this had little impact on the competitive side of things. Critically the game was liked, but many felt it was one of the weaker entries in the series, especially as the multiplayer aspect felt very similar to the previous year's *Black Ops 3*.

As an esport the game worked incredibly well, as with most other titles in the series. The action was quick-paced and required a lot of skill and fast reaction times from players if they wanted to do well. Some argued that this took away from the tactical side too much, but it did make the action very exciting.

However, there was one issue that dominated much of the season. A bug in the game, which became known as snaking, allowed players to look over certain objects without being seen by opponents. This was done by constantly going from prone to standing while moving in a circular direction, and in certain locations it could provide quite the advantage. It was eventually patched out of the game, but not before many teams had used it to win crucial games.

The season was also one of the most competitive seen for some time. The two biggest names in *Call of Duty*, OpTic Gaming and FaZe Clan,

impressed as usual, but other names such as eUnited and Splyce found themselves winning major international events as well. The *Infinite Warfare* season was also credited with being one of the first where EU teams could realistically challenge NA teams at every event, with many teams performing well across all of the big tournaments.

WW2

After *Infinite Warfare's* average critical reception and a lot of backlash from fans, Activision chose to return to a historical setting for the 2017 release of *Call of Duty*. The setting chosen was World War II, with *Call of Duty: WW2* releasing in November 2017. This was the first time in years that the series had gone back to a historical setting: they'd usually favored modern-day and futuristic settings since *Black Ops* in 2010.

The game was a complete overhaul of the *Call of Duty* formula. Since the release of *Advanced Warfare* in 2014 the systems used in the games had felt very similar, with the advanced movement in play. All of that was removed for *WW2*, with a return to boots-on-the-ground combat, which was designed to be more in line with the actual combat in WWII. This of course impacted many areas of the multiplayer side of things, the pace of the game slowed down significantly and a more tactical style of play returned.

The general consensus is good. Fans have wanted a return to this style of gameplay for a long time, and while the core game is very different from the last few years, the action that has made the game popular as an esport is still present. Things are certainly looking very good for the *Call of Duty* **scene** right now!

MLG

Before Activision took control of the *CoD* esports **scene** it was event organizer MLG who held most of the top-level competitions. In 2016 Activision purchased MLG for $46 million and now uses the company to run most of the pro-level *CoD* competitions in North America.

HALO 5

As you might expect from a series as iconic as *Halo*, people have been playing it competitively for years. Well before the esports boom, *Halo* tournaments were commonplace, and in the early days it really was one of the premier esports. While the **grassroots** tournaments were common in the early *Halo* titles, it was MLG who really led the way. They were organizing major events with the original *Halo*, with prize pools hitting the tens of thousands, which was rare back then.

IT was with the release of *Halo 2* that things really kicked up a notch. MLG once again led the way and supported the game pretty much from day one. They held regular events in the US and continued to increase prize pools. By 2005 they had put up $55,000 at one event, and then in 2006 they bumped that up to a massive $180,000.

The MLG *Halo 3* competitions of the late 2000s are a big part of what really pushed the industry to another level. *Halo 3* proved to be massively successful on the Xbox 360, and the esports side of *Halo* benefited hugely from this. More viewers tuned in, and everything started to grow rapidly. MLG hosted $56,000 events multiple times a year, and grew their end-of-year event prize pools to $280,000 by 2008.

MLG continued to support *Halo* until the end of the *Halo Reach* season, but once *Halo 4* hit, MLG's support dropped off as they focused on other esports games, and the **scene** was struggling. The *Halo 4* Global Championship was one of the first events to be supported by developer 343 Industries and had a $300,000 prize pool, but the **scene** seemed to be on its last legs.

THE HALO CHAMPIONSHIP SERIES

With the *Halo* **scene** struggling after *Halo 4*, developer 343 realized they needed to do something to try and reenergize the community. This came in the form of the *Halo* Championship Series, which was announced in 2014. The competition was initially for the remaster of *Halo 2*, which inspired a lot of old pro players to return. The HCS offered regular matches with top broadcast production and big prize pools. $300,000 was handed out during the *Halo 2* Anniversary HCS season, and it looked like *Halo* was again on the up.

Things continued to improve when *Halo 5 Guardians* was released in 2015. The HCS circuit was expanded and more money was invested, partly thanks to the success that rival publisher Activision found with its *Call of Duty* World League, and Microsoft wanting to challenge them. Viewership exploded and *Halo* was once again massively popular.

The introduction of the *Halo* World Championship also helped out in a big way. The 2016 iteration featured a partly crowd-funded prize pool and it hit a massive $2,500,000, making it the biggest *Halo* event in history. This kind of money brought in even more viewers, and the event itself can only be considered an unqualified success.

The HCS has certainly saved pro *Halo*, and right now the **scene** is as healthy as ever. This year has seen a bit of a drop-off thanks to some controversial tournament formats, and of course the lack of a new game to play, but the first issue has already been resolved and we probably aren't far away from the second being fixed too. When the next *Halo* releases, there is no reason the HCS couldn't challenge the CWL to become the largest console-shooter esports league.

GEARS OF WAR

While the other major console shooters, such as *Call of Duty* and *Halo*, have been around since the early 2000s or before, *Gears of War* didn't show up until much later. The first game in the series launched in 2006, and quickly became an iconic Xbox 360 exclusive title. The third-person shooter's **cover-based** mechanics were crafted to such a high quality, that it was one of the best shooters ever made, and the online portion wasn't half bad either.

WHILE the multiplayer mode in the first *Gears of War* game felt a bit like a tacked-on extra to some players, it actually functioned pretty well. The fast-paced mature nature of the gameplay, combined with the often very-close-quarters combat fighting, allowed for some massive plays, and this meant no round was truly over until the last man went down.

GEARS OF WAR PRO CIRCUIT

Fortunately, with *Gears of War 4*, Microsoft decided it wanted to revitalize the pro *Gears of War* **scene**. So, much like it did with *Halo* and the *HCS*, the *Gears of War* Pro Circuit was formed. The competition was announced in August 2016, a few months before *Gears of War 4* launched, and things got started from day one of the game's life on shelves. Players initially competed in online ladders and tournaments on the GameBattles platform to secure points.

MLG picked the game up for two seasons in 2007 and 2008, with prize pools going as high as $70,000. At the time it was up there with the big titles in terms of viewership and interest, and everything looked good.

But once *Gears of War 2* rolled around in late 2008, everything changed. The balance of the multiplayer meant that quick, close-quarters combat was too risky, and the pace slowed down. Frequent patches also constantly changed the game and upset a number of pros. It enjoyed some time on the MLG circuit, but was quickly cut, and *Gears* esports became a much smaller affair with almost all competition taking place online.

Gears of War 3 did little to change this, and the subsequent *Gears of War: Judgement* and remastered Xbox One version of the original game didn't really have much in the way of big esports **scenes**.

The top players would then be flown to **LAN** events around the world, which were hosted by MLG and Gfinity. All of these events were open, so anyone could sign up and compete against the top players, creating quite an incredible atmosphere.

The combination of online and **LAN** events meant that the total prize pool for the first year of competition was $1,000,000. This was the kick start that the scene needed. Players returned and a lot of new ones entered the scene. While it had been on life support for some time, the Pro Circuit brought it back with a bang, and now the future looks good for the first time in years. It also helps that *Gears of War 4*'s multiplayer was well-balanced and suited to competitive play.

RAINBOW SIX SIEGE

Rainbow Six Siege launched back in 2015 and was considered a solid game that did a lot well, but a number of factors led to a difficult launch. Tech issues combined with tragic real world events limited what the marketing team could do. This meant that in its first few months, *Rainbow Six Siege* did not do as well as Ubisoft had hoped.

BUT those who did play the game loved it, and quickly started to request competitive events. Ubisoft partnered with ESL to run the *Rainbow Six* Pro League and competitions were formed. With some solid money on the line and each season (of which there are four each year) having a **LAN** final, some big name organizations got involved.

The **scene** continued to grow throughout the first year and had a massive impact on the game itself. As the esports side of things became more popular, more and more people started to buy the game, with massive player spikes around key events.

The first year of pro play ended with the Six Invitational, a world championship event in Montreal, Canada. The event was a massive success, hitting 120,000 concurrent viewers at one point, which is a lot better than many major esports events usually do.

One of the reasons *Siege* has managed to do so well is down to its unique gameplay. It's a **first-person shooter** that is a lot more tactical than *CoD* and *CS:GO*. One team must try and break into a building, while the other sets up in defensive positions to stop them. Each character in the game has a unique ability and different weapons, which means there is also an element of the **MOBA** or hero shooter here as well.

The Six Invitational was the first world championship event for *Rainbow Six Siege*, with the top teams from all regions heading to Montreal, Canada, to battle it out for a share of $200,000. The event featured competitions for both the Xbox One and PC versions of the game, with the prize pool being split equally between the two.

The three-day event saw teams battle it out in front of a massive crowd, as well as a lot of panels from the developers during the downtime. New **DLC** and other announcements were made, and there were a few extra surprises, such as appearances from the voice actors in the game.

On the PC side of things it was Continuum who were crowned champions, while on the Xbox One it was Elevate. In the PC finals it looked like Continuum were heading for a loss on multiple occasions, but in the

final few rounds they turned it around to send eRa Eternity home in second place.

The event was a massive success, showcasing how *Rainbow Six* has managed to establish itself as one of the top esports out there. It is expected that when the event returns in 2018, the viewer numbers will once again break industry records.

OPERATION HEALTH

Earlier this year the *Rainbow Six Siege* developers delayed the release of some new **DLC** characters to focus on improving the health of the game. This included a number of bug fixes and performance enhancements, making the game a lot smoother and more reliable. It's rare that a developer will delay **DLC** to improve the base game, so Ubisoft should be applauded for this move.

NOTABLE WORLD CHAMPIONS

EVIL GENIUSES
THE INTERNATIONAL 5 (2015)

Evil Geniuses (EG) have long been the best *DotA 2* team in North America. Ever since the organization picked up the S A D B O Y S team in early 2014, which featured Clinton "Fear" Loomis, Artour "Arteezy" Babaev, Saahil "UNiVeRsE" Arora, Ludwig "zai" Wåhlberg and Peter "ppd" Dager, the organization has dominated the NA **scene**. In fact since then EG has always been a top-five team in the world, despite quite a few roster changes.

Heading into TI4 these players were considered the favorites despite it being their first TI together. They performed OK, coming third, and took home over $1,000,000. But this wasn't enough for them—they wanted more. The next twelve months would be strange for EG. Zai and Arteezy left to join Team Secret, so EG brought in Kurtis "Aui_2000" Ling and new kid on the block Syed Sumail "SumaiL" Hassan.

This team would enter TI5 as a favorite, and this time things were different. EG stormed to the winners' bracket final, where they faced Chinese side CDEC. EG were dominated in this one, losing 2–0 in quick fashion. They quickly bounced back in the lower bracket to set up the rematch in the finals.

The finals were incredibly close, but EG won, thanks to an iconic echo-slam play from UNiVeRsE and ppd. They took home more than $6 million and became the first NA team to win The International. This established them as one of the best esports teams of all time.

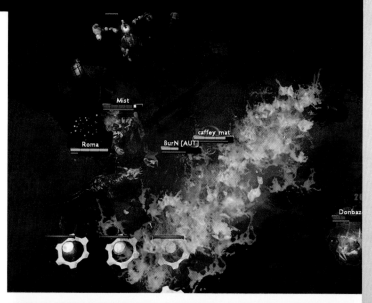

SK TELECOM T1
LEAGUE OF LEGENDS (2013, 2015, 2016)

Esports players don't get any more dominant than SK Telecom T1 (SKT). The South Korean team has won the *League of Legends* world championship three times in four years, making them without doubt the best *League of Legends* team to date.

For every one of their three championship wins the team has been slightly different, but both Bae "Bengi" Seong-woong and Lee "Faker" Sang-hyeok have been on the team for all three wins. After the first win this duo could bring in whatever players they liked, with everyone wanting to play with them. Faker is widely regarded as the best player in the world, so almost everyone was eager to play with him.

As the rosters changed, the success didn't really go away. They weren't world champions in 2014, but they came back strong in 2015. They destroyed all non-Korean teams convincingly, and managed to beat their fellow countrymen whenever they met.

The same was true in 2016, when SKT only lost two maps to non-Korean opponents in the entire competition. Their semifinal match against fellow Koreans Rox Tigers will go down as one of the best series in *League of Legends* history, and the final against the other Korean team, Samsung Galaxy, is a must-watch. SKT's dominance in the world of *LoL* is incredible, and there is a very good chance that no other team will ever match their accomplishments.

NOTABLE WORLD CHAMPIONS

GAMBIT ESPORTS
CS:GO (2017)

Heading into the second *CS:GO* Major of 2017, there were a few teams that most people thought had a very good chance of winning. SK Gaming had been on an incredible three-event winning streak, Astralis were the reigning champions (and even skipped a $250,000 **LAN** to save **strats**), G2 were the French superteam capable of beating anyone, and FaZe had the most firepower in the world. Very few expected that Gambit Esports would walk out as champions.

But that is exactly what they did. The CIS team stayed strong as more and more big names dropped out. They beat G2 in the group stage and Astralis in the semifinal before meeting Brazilian team Immortals in the final. The final itself was pretty close, but eventually Gambit came out on top to become the *CS:GO* World Champions.

This huge win will go down in the history books for a number of reasons. This certainly isn't the first time that an underdog has won a Major, and it probably won't be the last, but it is important. Their win proved that you don't necessarily need a star player to build a team around, and that an opposition team's unique style of play can still be bested by a good **in-game leader**.

It is quite possible that good **in-game leaders** will start to command ridiculous salaries and contracts, purely because it is now very difficult for a team to win without one. When Zeus was kicked from NaVi he ended up on the pretty-unknown Gambit, with few other offers. Now the chances of something like that happening to a top **IGL** again are next to none.

DU "NUCKLEDU" DANG
STREET FIGHTER V (2016)

The first Capcom Cup for *Street Fighter V* featured all of the big names you could imagine. But more than a few of them went out in the early rounds. The top-seeded player, Lee "Infiltration" Seon-woo, went out in joint last place, with many other top seeds following him.

American player Du "NuckleDu" Dang, who was ranked fourth coming into the event, managed to avoid these embarrassing results, continuing to make his way through the winners' bracket, and making it all the way to the final without losing a game. In the final he met fellow American Ricki Ortiz, who was ranked 26th coming into the event. Ricki had proved that she was up there with the best of them, but unfortunately NuckleDu was just too strong in the final.

The win meant that NuckleDu was the first-ever world champion for *Street Fighter V*, which is quite the honor. His win sent out a message to the rest of the world: when it comes to these big events, anyone can win, and the favorites are certainly not guaranteed anything. This is a trend that has continued in the world of *Street Fighter*, and one that makes it super-exciting to watch.

SPEEDRUNNING

Speedrunning is the art of completing a game as fast as possible. It really is that simple: players spend years learning how to complete a game in the fastest time possible. Official world records are recorded, and the players, also known as runners, complete runs, trying to beat the times of their counterparts.

UNLIKE most esports, there isn't much in the way of direct competition. Most runs are done at home with streams, and rarely do multiple people try to run the same game at the same time. While any game can be speedrun, there is a selection of games that are more suitable to it. These are usually single-player story-based campaigns, and there is no real age limit, so some of the most popular titles to run are NES and SNES games.

The premier speedrunning events are the biannual Games Done Quick streams. These events take place in a hotel in the US and feature a 24/7 stream for the best part of a week. Awesome Games Done Quick (AGDQ) takes place in early January of each year and Summer Games Done Quick (SGDQ) usually takes place in July, with hundreds of runners pitching games that they want to run at the event. Once the final list has been decided, the runners jump on a couch with other runners to show off their best speed. They run and talk viewers through what they are doing.

The events are to raise money for charity. AGDQ raises money for the Prevent Cancer Foundation, while SGDQ raises money for Doctors without Borders. AGDQ 2017 raised $2,222,791 while SGDQ 2017 raised $1,781,480 for the respective charities.

METROID PRIME

DOOM

When the community identifies a new game that they want to try and run, they will all band together to try to find the hidden secrets. Often they will find some kind of crazy skip that allows them to cut out massive chunks of the game. Often these skips are so niche and hard to do that the developers will leave them in the game.

Even if a skip is not involved, the community will spend hours finding the optimal way to beat the game. They may find nonstandard movement techniques that make moving through areas a tiny bit quicker, or they may find a way to defeat a boss without it getting off a potentially run-ending attack. Sometimes they will find tricks that

can only be performed on an exact frame of a game, which means their reaction time needs to be incredible. Sometimes these tricks may only save a handful of frames, but it's all the small things that shave off seconds at final time.

The speedrunning community is a very close-knit group, and while it isn't as big as the major esports out there, it is one of the most active communities. While many people will run a game or two, they will also watch and participate in runs of other games, and for the most part everyone seems to get along well with each other.

THE LEGEND OF ZELDA: OCARINA OF TIME

FIFA

The world of *FIFA* esports has truly exploded in the last few years, and it is still growing, meaning that it has the potential to become one of the biggest esports in the world. But while this increase in popularity is a new occurrence, *FIFA* has been a pretty big esport for years.

EVER since esports really became a thing in the early 2000s, people have been playing *FIFA* competitively, and even before then people would organize tournaments with friends around the very early releases in the '90s. When the first rounds of investment came into esports *FIFA* was often there. It was a core part of the Championship Gaming Series, the short-lived competitive gaming league that was broadcast on national TV in the US and UK. Big organizers from that period such as WCG and ESWC often ran events with thousands of dollars up for grabs.

Finesse Shot **RB** +
Chip Shot **LB** +

Some say that in recent years the FIFA Interactive World Cup (FIWC) has struggled to keep up with the *FIFA* **scene** and it's reluctant to adopt the **FIFA Ultimate Team game mode**. Despite all of the issues 2016's final was one of the most hyped *FIFA* matches of all time. UK player Sean "Dragon" Allen was winning until the final minutes, when Mohamad "Al-Bacha" Al-Bacha came back and took the win in dramatic fashion.

Outside of the FIWC, developers EA have recently taken control of a lot of the **scene**. The *FIFA* 17 Ultimate Team Championship is now the official competition in the world of *FIFA* and is led by EA. While they haven't been the most hands-on publisher in the world previously, they have done a solid job with this event, taking the game

mode that the pros most like to play and creating an interesting format around it. All of the **LAN** events have been solid, and the unique idea of having the winners of the Xbox and PS4 competitions play each other for the overall championship as the final match is a nice twist.

Recent years have seen major soccer teams sign *FIFA* pro gamers, with interest in the **scene** growing a lot as a result. While a lot of teams in other sports are investing in esports in general, soccer teams seem to want to stick to what they know and only sign *FIFA* pro gamers. Outside of a few notable examples such as Paris Saint-Germain, most teams have only ventured into *FIFA* for the time being. However, this has been seen as a good thing and has a lot of people very excited about the future of the *FIFA* **scene**.

The *FIFA* Interactive World Cup has been running for thirteen years, and has been recognized by the Guinness World Records as the biggest gaming tournament in the world on multiple occasions. In the early days the tournament was pretty small, but now it has become a massive fixture in the *FIFA* calendar. While the prize pool has stayed at $26,000 for some time, the 2017 iteration bumped this up so that the winner took home $200,000.

MADDEN

Madden has been a massive success and competitive esport in the US for years. Outside of the US, many have never heard of it, but in the States, it's one of the true pioneers.

A S with most sports games, there was a **grassroots scene** across the US in the early-to-mid 2000s. Local players would compete in unofficial competitions and while concrete information on these events is limited, they did seem to be quite widespread and popular.

Then in 2005 the big names really got involved. ESPN created a reality TV show called *Madden Nation* with EA and the NFL. This show was aired on ESPN2 and saw a number of top *Madden* players compete for $100,000. The show turned out to be pretty successful and ran for four seasons. This was one of the first times that esports really worked in a traditional TV broadcast and is seen as one of the pioneers of esports on TV.

Since then *Madden* has always had strong support from a number of parties, including EA, but only in recent years has it really risen to the mainstream consciousness outside of the States. When EA announced its new competitive gaming division, the *Madden* **scene** was again thrust into the spotlight. EA now hosts regular top-level *Madden* competitions and things seem to be on the up again. Interest outside the US is still limited, but things are looking good.

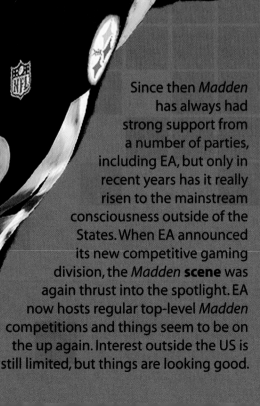

MADDEN 17

There is no doubt that the *Madden 17* season was one of the most successful years yet for the new-look *Madden* **scene**. EA really upped its commitment to the game and the events were bigger than ever. Throughout the year there were four major events: the *Madden* Classic, *Madden* Bowl, *Madden* Challenge, and *Madden* Championship.

These events featured play across a number of game modes and some pretty sizable prize pools at the **LAN** finals. $100,000 was up for grabs at the first event, with that rising to $500,000 for the *Madden* Championship at the end of the season.

These big events had some issues, such as the champion of the *Madden* Bowl, Chris "Dubby" McFarland being fined $3,000 for inappropriate tweets, which resulted in a lot of negative coverage. But overall the season can be considered a big success.

The end-of-year *Madden* Championship was one of the biggest *Madden* events ever, and brought in thousands of viewers. Michael Skimbo ended up winning the competition and became the *Madden* World Champion. He will be looking to defend that crown next season on *Madden 18*.

NBA2K

In the US the *NBA2K* series has been one of the best-selling franchises for years. Ever since the mid-2000s, the franchise has undoubtedly been the best basketball game out there and in recent years some have said that it has been the best sports simulation game, period. A high-quality title that allows for competition is always going to become an esport, and that is exactly what happened to *NBA2K*.

WHILE there has always been a competitive **scene**, it's only been in the last couple of years that things have taken off for *NBA2K*. Last year 2K hosted the *NBA2K* Road to the Finals event, where teams of five players would compete on the digital court. The winners walked away with both $250,000 and a ticket to the NBA finals.

After the success of that competition, the NBA and 2K are now forming the *NBA2K* esports league, which launched its first season on May 1, 2018. NBA teams will sign the top players in the world, and they will compete against other teams in the league.

If this league turns out to be a success then it wouldn't be a surprise to see *NBA2K* sit at the top of the sports world alongside *FIFA*. If it turns out to be an **XFL-style failure**, then who knows what the future holds for the series.

The *NBA2K* league is still in its early development stage, but is already quite an exciting prospect. At least seventeen of the main NBA teams will sign some *NBA2K* players and compete against each other.

The Boston Celtics, Cleveland Cavaliers, Dallas Mavericks, Detroit Pistons, Golden State Warriors, Indiana Pacers, Memphis Grizzlies, Miami Heat, Milwaukee Bucks, New York Knicks, Orlando Magic, Philadelphia 76ers, Portland Trail Blazers, Sacramento Kings, Toronto Raptors, Utah Jazz and Washington Wizards are the first teams to get involved and have agreed to at least three years of the league. Many of those teams, or the team owners, have already dipped a toe into the world of esports, so it is no surprise to see some of the names in there.

A player selection is expected to happen after some kind of scouting to determine the gamers that teams will pick up. That means you still have a chance to get involved if you find yourself winning more than a few games online in *NBA2K* 18!

DIGNITAS

In 2016, the Philadelphia 76ers, a top NBA team, purchased both the Team Dignitas and Apex Gaming organizations, combining them under the Dignitas name. The 76ers now feature the Dignitas logo on the team's jerseys.

PES

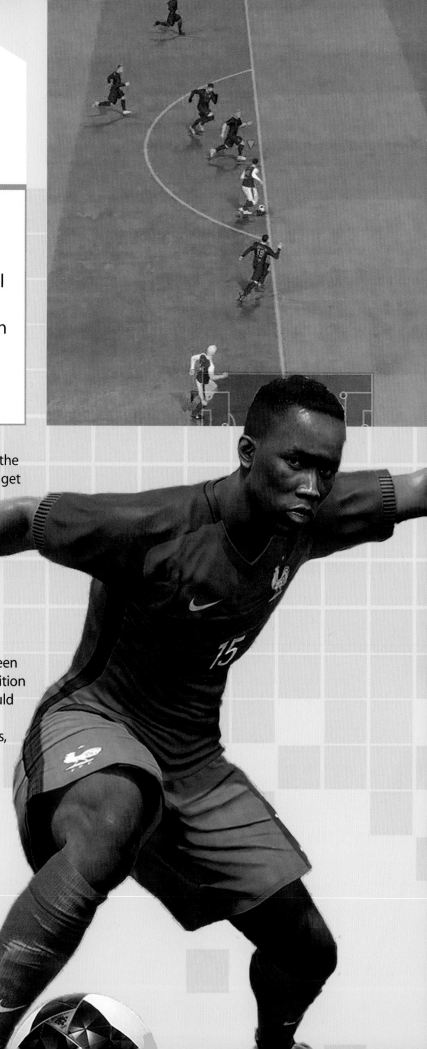

Pro Evolution Soccer (PES) has been the main competitor for *FIFA* for years. In the early-to-mid 2000s it was clear that *PES* was a much better game, but without real team licenses it often struggled in terms of sales. In recent years *PES* has once again managed to challenge *FIFA* in the game-play department and is slowly but surely securing more licenses.

IN terms of the esports **scene,** it has only been in the last few years where things have really started to get big for *PES*. Konami has long supported esports and has often tied the events into the Champions League finals, thanks to a license deal in the game, but prize pools remained small for quite a while.

But in recent years the prize pool for *PES* League has been expanded massively. For the *PES 17* season the competition followed a similar format to previous years. Players would compete online, with the best making it to national finals. The winners would then make it to regional finals, where the money really kicked in. Each regional final had $40,000 up for grabs and qualification for the world finals, which turned out to be the biggest *PES* event ever.

All eyes now turn to the 2018 season and of course the recently released *PES 2018*. While the game itself may not have all of the fancy broadcast style and official license of *FIFA*, when it comes down to pure competition the gameplay allows for such a high level that you totally forget that you might be watching Man Red instead of Manchester United.

PES LEAGUE
ROAD TO CARDIFF

presented by **KONAMI**

ROAD TO CARDIFF

The 2017 *PES* League was known as the Road to Cardiff, as the winner was presented with the trophy at the Champions League Final in Cardiff, Wales. The actual finals of the competition took place at the Emirates Stadium in London, Arsenal's stadium, a few days before the Champions League Final. The 2017 *PES* League world finals featured the biggest ever *PES* prize pool. The winner walked away with a massive $200,000, with second taking $100,000 and third $50,000. In previous years the total for the world finals didn't break the $30,000 mark!

The finals were a very worldwide affair, with players from all over the world competing to become world champion and $200,000 richer. It was the South Americans who dominated the tournament, in what turned out to be a pretty unpredictable event!

LUIS "JHONA_KRA" SALAZAR

Peruvian "Jhona_Kra" took third place, worth $50,000.

ETTORE "ETTORITO97" GIANNUZZI

Born in Italy, "Ettorito97" was the only non-South American to win some cash, taking second place worth $100,000.

GUILHERME "GUIFERA" FONSECA

"GuiFera" took the big prize of $200,000 home to Brazil.

10 AWESOME JOBS IN ESPORTS

COMMUNITY MANAGER

The job of the community manager is pretty much just to post on social media (which we all do most days) so this is a pretty sweet gig. Community managers are needed for all esports organizations. This role involves keeping fans up to date with what is going on, and being the voice of the organization. Many community managers gain a large personal following, which can be very useful in other future roles. You'll have to have a thick skin though, as internet commenters can be the worst…

TEAM COACH

If you have some incredible game knowledge but just aren't quite good enough to go pro, then being a coach is for you. The coach has differing roles depending on the team and the game, but for the most part they will be the one working with the players on strategies and how to improve. Most games allow coaches to stand behind the team on stage, meaning you will get some popularity, but you also don't have to be the world's best player. Coaches can also make quite a bit of money, so if you're good, it could become very lucrative.

TEAM MANAGER

The team manager is the person who makes sure the team has everything they need. The exact roles will vary from organization to organization, but for the most part it will involve sorting travel, organizing boot camps, making sure players have a schedule and knowing when their games are, and other admin tasks. The manager's job is to make sure that the team is as comfortable as possible so they can do their job. One perk of this is that most managers get to go with the teams to events, so you will get to travel the world!

TEAM CHEF

Not all teams will have a dedicated chef, but there are quite a few out there, and it is a growing field. Team chefs will head to the team house, sometimes even live there and cook all the meals for the players. The role is much more than this though. The chef will also have to come up with balanced diets that will help the players perform to their maximum. For anyone who has some cooking skills and wants to work in esports, this is a dream job.

JOURNALIST

There are many types of esports journalists in the world, but for the most part their job is to tell the stories that go on in the esports **scene**. Most will pick one game and become an expert in that, allowing them to do analysis of matches and tournaments, as well as tell the wider stories. Others will choose to follow multiple games telling the bigger stories across all of the games. Some of the top journalists in the world get to attend all of the big events and interview the players, so if you want to meet your heroes then this is a good way of doing it. There is, however, a lot of competition in this field…

PR REP

A PR (Public Relations) rep is a person who deals with the media and sends out press releases. Teams rarely have a dedicated PR rep, but tournament organizers and developers certainly will. A lot of the job is coordinating with media outlets to make sure they get what they need, but a PR rep also writes announcements about their organization and works on marketing efforts. Being a PR rep is not an easy role, but getting a gig at the right place can mean you can travel the world and attend all the big events.

VIDEO EDITOR

A good video editor is like gold dust in the world of esports. With everything revolving around online video content, having a good editor is key, as it can make your stuff stand out above the rest. Almost every organization will need a video editor to create some kind of content, so there are a lot of opportunities out there. But to get a full-time gig you will have to prove that you are great at what you do, and can produce some of the best videos in the entire **scene**.

STREAMER

Being a streamer isn't strictly related to esports, but many of the big organizations hire full-time streamers, whose sole job is to play games and let people watch. This is because sponsors will want a certain amount of time where their logo or ad is shown, and to make sure that happens organizations hire streamers who will stream with these advertisements on. Unfortunately you can't just walk into a streaming job, you will have to have a decent following beforehand, and if you want to do this you will have to put in a lot of unpaid hours. Even then it is far from guaranteed.

Being a game developer is not a single role, it is made up of hundreds of smaller roles, from programmer to level designer to charter artist and many, many more. However, it is a way that you get to work in esports and be a part of one of the coolest areas, actually making the games. Without developers there would be no esports, and just think: it could be you that makes the next major esport that gives hundreds of people a job.

GAME DEVELOPER

PRODUCTION CREW

Like game developers, being a part of the production crew is not just one job, but without them the esports industry wouldn't exist. The production crew is made up of everything from stage managers to camera operators, IT technicians, and every other broadcast role under the sun. These are the people who make sure events happen and broadcasts run with no technical issues, so that we all get to experience the massive events that esports is known for.

THE NEXT WAVE

YOU FRAGGED Smokey65

SUMMARY SCORE: 1
SUMMARY XP: 5
KILL: 5

QUAKE CHAMPIONS

Quake is one of the original esports. Back in the day it was up there with the big games when it came to massive tournaments, and some of the biggest names in the industry got their start in *Quake*. But the series has been dormant for quite a few years, missing the esports boom entirely!

Now the classic shooter is back, and it has changed quite a bit. The core fast-paced first-person gameplay returns, but this time it has taken some inspiration from *Overwatch* and introduced a string of different heroes. Each of these heroes has one active ability and one passive. The active abilities range from covering everything in front of you in acid to being able to see through walls, and it changes things a lot. No longer is *Quake* just about who has the best shooting ability; you

now have to factor in character match-ups and when to use those all-important abilities.

That being said, there is still a lot of original *Quake* action on offer here. The movement feels very similar to the original titles that everyone loved back in the day, and the shooting is near identical. As ever, you still have to run around the map to grab stronger weapons, and cool gameplay features such as rocket jumping still exist.

Quake Champions already has a bit of an esports **scene**, with publisher Bethesda hosting the $1,000,000 world championships at QuakeCon this year. However, it is still very early on and it remains to be seen how well *Quake Champions* will do going forward.

LAWBREAKERS

LawBreakers is the latest game from Cliff Bleszinski, the man who was a lead developer of *Gears of War* and many other iconic titles. After leaving *Gears* developer Epic Games, he set up his own studio to build *LawBreakers*, with the game launching in August 2017. Reception to the game was pretty good, but it struggled early on in terms of player numbers, casting a doubt on its esports potential.

The game is a **first-person shooter** that features multiple heroes, just like seemingly every other shooter released in 2017. The hero roster is a little more limited than most, but the variety in their abilities makes that a less painful pill to swallow. The real interesting point of *LawBreakers* is the maps and the gravity-defying areas they have. Different maps work differently, but for the most part they will have an area or two of low gravity, which instantly adds extra vertical layers to the combat.

We have yet to see how the game fares in the world of esports. It certainly has the potential, and some of the online games are often incredibly close, which adds a lot of positives for it to succeed as a spectator sport. At the moment it has a fairly small player base, but with a little more time and a few gameplay **balance changes**, it could become quite a successful new esport title . . .

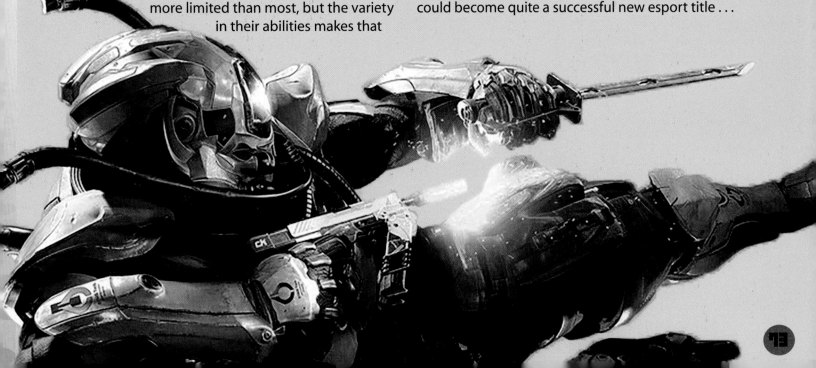

PLAYERUNKNOWN'S BATTLEGROUNDS

PlayerUnknown's Battlegrounds (PUBG) was the most successful game of 2017 by far. Within a few months of launching, it became the third-most-popular game on Steam ever, only being beaten by *DotA 2* and *CS:GO,* and it has sold over four million copies. Even during its early-access days **LAN** events were happening, some with more than $300,000 on offer.

The game sees up to 100 people drop onto an island filled with weapons. You start with nothing and have to loot buildings to get a usable arsenal that can take down others. The winner is the last player standing (or team if you play with friends), so you must eliminate the other players on the island. To stop this from becoming a total camp fest where everyone just hides in a building, a circular force field slowly forces players together. Straying outside the safe area for too long will kill you and bring your round to an end.

With ninety-nine other people to take down, winning a game really does feel like quite the accomplishment, and while there is some **RNG** in terms of loot generation, this mostly comes down to skill. You have to learn when to take fights, when to run away, when to hide, and how

to engage, and there are hundreds of variables to all of these things. For what is a pretty simple concept, there is a lot of depth here.

The game launched with third-person servers only, but first-person servers were added a few months into the game's life. These servers kept everything the exact same, except for the viewpoint, which changed how the game is played significantly. The community still seems to be split on which it prefers, but with millions of players that really isn't an issue.

When *PUBG* first launched it became a big hit with many of the biggest **Twitch** streamers, and the game would often outperform the biggest esports on the streaming service, showing that people were prepared to watch it. Online-only competitions then really took off; they were difficult thanks to the limited **spectator mode**, but after a while the quality improved and they became really good events to watch.

Then at Gamescom in August 2017, ESL and developers Bluehole hosted the *PUBG* Invitational that saw some of the best players in the world compete for a share of

$350,000. This is when the world really saw what *PUBG* was capable of in a competitive setting, and it worked out well. The viewing figures were very good and feedback was mostly positive, showing that there is certainly a lot of interest in future competitions.

Right now it seems inevitable that *PUBG* will become a top esport in the next few years. Prize pools are already beating some of the tier-two esports, and some massive organizations such as Team Liquid, TSM and Cloud9 all have *PUBG* teams. This one is more of a case of how long it will take to reach the top rather than if it will ever reach the top, and that certainly isn't a bad thing.

SPLATOON 2

When Nintendo first showed off the Nintendo Switch, a big portion of the reveal trailer showed off the possibilities of the console in the world of esports, with the portability making it easy for events to change between matches quickly and easily. We have yet to see that kind of event happen, but *Splatoon 2* is starting to make some waves in the competitive world.

Splatoon is technically a shooter, but it is a very Nintendo shooter that is designed for a family audience. Instead of bullets, the ammo is paint and the aim of the game is to try to paint as much of the map in your color as possible. The team with the most painted areas at the end of the match wins. Covering your enemy in paint will kill them and send them back to the spawn point, giving you some extra time to get some paint uncontested. It really is much more fun than it sounds on paper, honest!

The first title was a surprise esports hit, with quite a few **LAN** competitions taking place. Prize pools were small but it was popular, and Nintendo clearly realized this.

While the **scene** is still young at this point, *Splatoon 2* is proving that it can do well as an esport. ESL has worked with Nintendo to host a **LAN**, and it would be a big surprise if Nintendo didn't continue to support it. Of course, it will never hit the heights of *Call of Duty*, but as a family-friendly esport that is very easy to understand there is nothing better out there.

MARVEL VS CAPCOM: INFINITE

The *Marvel vs Capcom* (*MvC*) series has long been a favorite in the fighting game community, and it seems that the new version, *Marvel vs Capcom: Infinite*, is no different. There is no doubt that this will become one of the top fighting-game esports in the world, and it seems that Capcom is prepared to support the title's esports **scene** in the same way that it has for *Street Fighter*.

The last *Marvel vs Capcom* game was released back in 2011, and was still around at **Evo**, the biggest fighting game tournament in the world, this year. There is a lot of love for *MvC*, and it would be a massive shock if this didn't turn out to be a hit in the **FGC**.

This version features a new tag-based combo system that allows players to switch between characters instantly, which can result in some incredible combo plays. It feels like the best players in the world are still learning some of the most effective ways to use this, so once they figure it all out this could be one of the most exciting fighting games to watch.

Given time, *Marvel vs Capcom: Infinite* will almost certainly be popping up at every major fighting game event, and probably bringing in some big crowds.

The franchise is loved by many, the Marvel characters bring in a mainstream interest, and the new systems means that this is some of the most exciting play we have ever seen. This one should be around for quite some time.

STREET FIGHTER V

When it comes to esports fighting games, there isn't any title bigger than *Street Fighter V*. Big events draw in thousands of participants and have massive prize pools, which means almost all the major esports organizations have a pro *Street Fighter* player or two. The action is simple to understand at a basic level, but almost impossible to truly master, which is what makes it a great spectator experience.

STREET *Fighter* has been played competitively for years, even when the very first games came out before online gaming even existed. Local communities formed to play tournaments with each other. Some larger events happened, but for the most part it was the same players from the same area playing against each other.

Of course the lack of online options meant that people had to play on the same screen, and some competitions were even held on arcade machines. This style of play is often still seen today, with many events having players compete shoulder to shoulder on the same screen. This gives a special feeling to the matches.

Street Fighter V (SFV) was released back in 2016, but there was a lot of backlash. The game launched in a difficult state, with a lot of features missing and a lot of controversial mechanics. However, a year of refinement and further development has made it into a very solid title, one that most people are really happy with. Initially there was some resistance to it replacing *Street Fighter IV* on the competitive circuit, but now it is the default title.

Capcom supported the title from day one, which didn't come as a surprise as they did the same thing for *Street Fighter IV* with the Capcom Pro Tour. This competition sees the publisher work with multiple third-party organizers to host events across the world. The players who perform well in these events across the year then qualify for the Capcom Cup, the annual world championship that had a massive $360,000 prize pool in 2016.

For the first time in 2016, Capcom also introduced some esports **DLC** to *Street Fighter*. A percentage of each sale of the **DLC** items contributed to the 2016 Capcom Cup prize pool, which is why it ended up being so large. Capcom did the same for the 2017 Capcom Cup.

While the Capcom Pro Tour events are what really matter in the world of *Street Fighter*, there are also a lot of other events going on all over the world. Most big events are incorporated into the tour, but outside of that things like the Gfinity Elite Series feature some of the best *SFV* talent competing on a weekly basis.

With a ton of publisher support, a stable **scene** that features many massive tournaments and its overall accessibility, *Street Fighter V* is rightfully up there as one of the biggest esports, and it shows no sign of slowing down anytime soon. Expect this one to be closing out the Capcom Cup for a long time to come.

STREET FIGHTER

 # CAPCOM PRO TOUR

The Capcom Pro Tour is the top competition in the world for *Street Fighter*, and runs throughout the year. Players compete at a number of partnered events and in some online competitions to earn points. At the end of the season, the players with the highest amount of points from the year will qualify for the Capcom Cup and have the chance to compete to become the World Champion.

The Pro Tour has been running since 2014, with Capcom refining the exact format every year. Previously winning a top event would automatically qualify a player for the Capcom Cup, which meant one good performance could secure you a place at the biggest event of the year. This proved controversial, so these days it is back to being those who perform best over the entire year.

Premier competitions are the big ones on the tour. These events usually take place at large esports events such as DreamHack Summer, massive gaming conventions such as EGX in the UK, or the biggest fighting-game specific tournaments such as CEO. **Evo** is classed as its own event, with the winner securing a massive amount of points that almost guarantees Capcom Cup qualification.

If you're new to the world of *Street Fighter* esports, then watching one of the premier events on the Pro Tour is the way to go. These competitions feature the best players and usually have great production compared with other events. Of course, the Capcom Cup at the end of the year is also a must-watch event!

TOP-TIER CHARACTERS

Street Fighter V was initially criticized for its seemingly lacking character roster, but thanks to some **DLC** releases there is now a pretty deep field of characters to choose from. This also means that there are a lot of options when it comes to choosing a character to **main** as you start your journey to the top. **Balance changes** do impact who is considered a top character quite often, but if you are looking to take on the pros, you can't go wrong with these options...

BALROG

Balrog is a boxer, and therefore a lot of his move set revolves around using his arms instead of his legs. He relies heavily on hitting quick but powerful punches to whittle down health bars, but is also capable of hitting some big combos if given the chance. He does resort to some tactics that would certainly get him banned in the world of boxing, but this is *Street Fighter* and anything goes ...

GUILE

Guile is a member of the American Air Force and has a very interesting skill set. Generally he is solid in most of the important areas, but the real way to master him is to learn how to counter others. Baiting opponents before counterattacking them is always a solid tactic for most, but for Guile it really works well. If you can get a good counter going, then a nice combo can be set up to end the round quickly. He's hard to learn, but it is very difficult to fight against a good Guile player.

CAMMY

Cammy has had a long history in the world of *Street Fighter* and a really complex back story. However, as a character in a competition she is fantastic for those who prefer a quicker style that can do a lot of damage in a short space of time. The idea is to catch your opponent off guard and then deliver a string of rapid attacks to bring them down. If you like quick action and have good reaction times, then this is the character for you!

INJUSTICE 2

Injustice 2 has already become one of the biggest fighting games in esports. The first game, which saw DC superheroes and villains fight against one another, was a big success, so a sequel was inevitable. This time a slightly different roster and some mechanical improvements resulted in a much-improved game, and the pro players instantly jumped on board.

JUST days after the game was released, publisher Warner Bros. launched the *Injustice 2* Pro Series, a long competition with events all over the world and a massive prize pool of $600,000. Initial stages saw regional events determine the best players, who then headed to LA for the finals in September, where more than $300,000 of the prize pool was up for grabs.

Outside of this series Warner Bros. has also been boosting the prize pools at major fighting-game events such as CEO and Combo Breaker, while other big events have also supported the game. **Evo** 2017 was the first time *Injustice 2* was played at the biggest fighting-game event of the year, and more than 800 people signed up for the competition. Eventually it was Ryan "Dragon" Walker who won, taking home over $35,000.

Injustice 2 is still very much in its early days, but there is no doubt that it will be one of the biggest fighting games out there for years to come. As often happens with NetherRealm titles, this will probably be the go-to game for many players until they release a new game, which won't be for years yet.

This means that the future is bright for *Injustice 2*, and with massive publisher support and a lot of goodwill in the wider community, it could realistically challenge *Street Fighter* for the number one spot in the esports fighting game **scene**.

MORTAL KOMBAT X

Before *Injustice 2* launched, *Mortal Kombat X* was the game of choice for these players. As the two are made by the same studio on the same engine, they are both mechanically very similar, meaning if you are good at one you are most likely just as good at the other. As we saw with the first *Injustice* and *Mortal Kombat* cycle, the pro players will always play the most recent game, which meant that *Mortal Kombat X* has now been phased out of most big competitions in favor of the new DC battler. But chances are in a few years a new *Mortal Kombat* title will roll around, and all those familiar faces will return once again …

SUPER SMASH BROS. MELEE

Super Smash Bros. Melee launched back in 2001, but is still one of the most popular esports games out there. The GameCube fighting title featuring iconic Nintendo characters has managed to withstand the test of time like no other game, and is still one of the most-watched fighting games on the **scene**. When it launched over fifteen years ago it was a huge hit, and small competitive **scenes** popped up around the world. After all, the game features no online play, meaning all tournaments had to be done locally.

DURING the early years of *Super Smash Bros.*, Major League Gaming supported the title a lot. Their events had the biggest prize pools, which at the time were some of the larger prize pools in all of esports. MLG's *Melee* singles and doubles competitions at the 2006 Las Vegas event are still the 15th and 16th biggest prize pools given out in any *Smash Melee* tournament, at $18,000 each. However, after a few years, MLG dropped support for the title and the **scene** shrank significantly.

The game began to decline in popularity and it was only the truly dedicated hardcore players who were still playing *Smash* by the late 2000s. There were still a lot of fans out there, but the game just couldn't compete with up-and-coming titles such as *League of Legends*. That all changed with **Evo** 2013.

Evo, the biggest fighting game tournament on the planet, is where all of the top titles in the genre go to crown their best players. For most titles it's almost like a pseudo world championship, but *Smash* had not been included for a few years. In 2013, the organizers ran a charity drive to decide the final game for the tournament. Fans could "vote" for their favorite to be included by donating money to the Breast Cancer Research Foundation. The game that raised the most money would be included at the event. *Smash* won by more than $15,000.

Melee being back at **Evo** proved one of the most popular games at the event. In fact it had the third-highest amount of sign-ups out of nine games. Add in an incredible battle between the top eight players in the competition, and the love for *Melee* had returned.

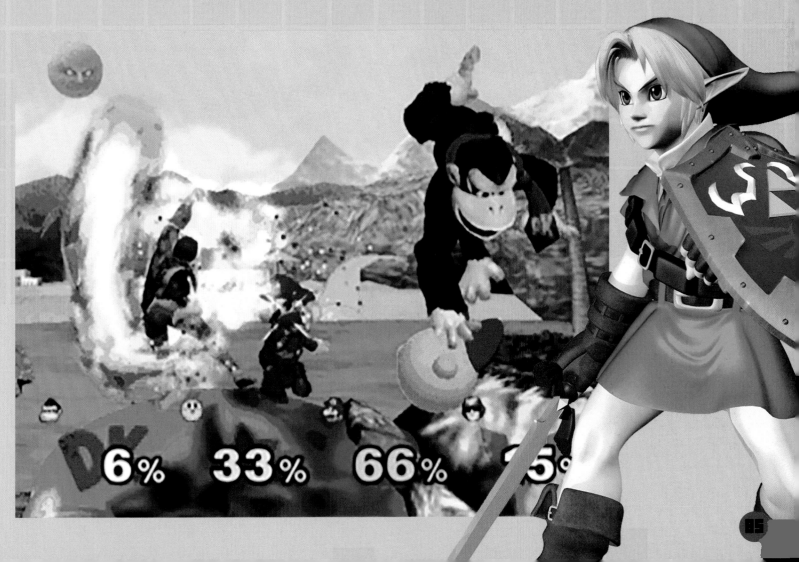

SUPER SMASH BROS. MELEE

This fan vote was the start of *Melee*'s resurgence and it has remained a fixture of **Evo** ever since. Many more tournaments have sprung up to support the **scene**, and it's more popular than ever. DreamHack has started to support the game with massive prize pools, and Beyond the Summit (a casting studio for *DotA*) decided to branch out its series of *DotA* events known as The Summit into the world of *Melee*. This has created some of the most lucrative events in the game's history.

These days *Melee* is one of the most popular fighting games out there, and while it is battling against the more recent *Super Smash Bros.* on Wii U, it is still holding strong and it seems like both games can coexist quite nicely.

THE FIVE GODS OF SMASH

In the more recent years of *Melee* there have been five players who have dominated the **scene**. These five are considered the best in the world and have won many events between them. If a premier event doesn't have one of these five gods in its top eight, then something has gone horribly wrong. While there are contenders for the sixth god throne, these are the five players who have dominated the *Melee* **scene** for years.

KEVIN "PPMD" NANNEY

Out of all the five gods, PPMD is probably the one who has struggled the most. In recent years he has played very few events and took a significant break from the **scene** in 2016. Only recently has he returned to top-level events, but he is still looking like one of the best out there. During his prime he was able to beat any of the other gods and took multiple tournament wins. He traditionally played using Falco, but also proved that Marth can be a top-level character as well.

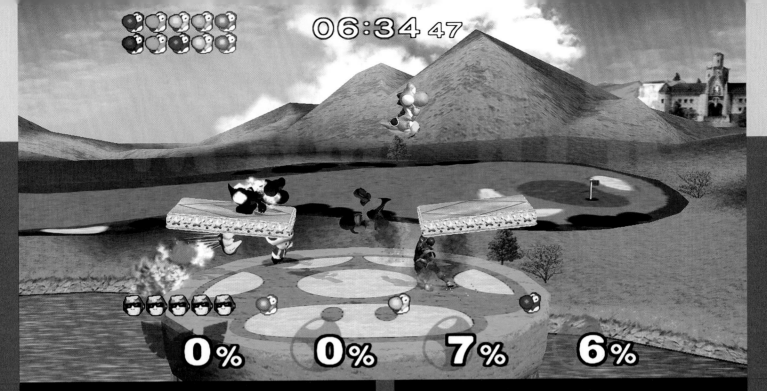

0%   0%   7%   6%

JASON "MEW2KING" ZIMMERMAN

Until recently, Mew2King was the highest-earning *Smash Bros.* player ever. While he has made a lot from *Melee*, he has also earned significant amounts in *Project M*, *Brawl* and even *Super Smash Bros.* on Wii U. But his real success came in *Melee*, where he has won a ton of events since starting out way back in 2005 as a sixteen-year-old. He is regarded as one of the smartest *Smash* players of all time, with a mechanical understanding that few can match, and is credited with discovering many aspects of *Melee*, such as weight and falling speed of characters.

JOSEPH "MANGO" MARQUEZ

Mango burst onto the **scene** way back in 2007 at **Evo**, when he defeated two of the best players at the time (Ken and Mew2King), and made the top three after seemingly coming from nowhere. Since then he has always been a threat, and right now is considered to be one of the two best players in the world. Mango was the one to win the massive comeback event at **Evo** 2013, and he managed to do the same thing again in 2014.

JUAN "HUNGRYBOX" DEBIEDMA

Hungrybox can certainly be described as a fan favorite when it comes to *Melee*. This is partly due to the fact that he is one of a small handful of top players that **main** Jigglypuff. Outside of Hungrybox, few others use the character as their primary fighter, but he has managed to make a name for himself by using the pink Pokémon. In recent years he has really kicked things up a notch, and right now looks to be a favorite for every tournament he takes part in.

ADAM "ARMADA" LINDGREN

Swedish player Armada is considered by most to be the best *Melee* player ever. He has won the most prize money in the game, and over the last few years has won more major events than anyone. These days, if Armada doesn't make the playoffs of an event then it has been a poor result for him, with almost every tournament he enters ending with a win. While there is still a long way to go before it can be truly decided, it does seem that Armada may be remembered as the best *Melee* player of all time when all is said and done.

SUPER SMASH BROS. WII U

Super Smash Bros. Wii U, or *Smash 4* as it has since become known, is the most recent release in the *Smash Bros.* franchise, having launched back in 2014. While the Wii U has since been replaced by the Nintendo Switch, the *Smash 4* competitive **scene** is bigger than ever, and for the first time *Smash 4* was the penultimate game at **Evo** on championship Sunday in 2017.

When it launched, many hoped that it would become the defacto *Smash* game and bring together the fractured communities of *Melee*, *Brawl* and *Project M*. That didn't happen, but arguably the system that we got is better than that. *Melee* continues to be its own beast and is doing very well, while *Smash 4* has become its own totally separate thing, with little crossover at the high levels. Both games get great support and are sustaining themselves comfortably.

AFTER its launch back in 2014, a competitive **scene** formed immediately. Most of the big-name players came from the struggling *Brawl* and *Project M* **scenes**, which had lost ground on *Melee* after its resurgence in early 2010. Early invitational tournaments were set up and by the time 2015 rolled around there was usually some kind of semi-big tournament going on every other week. Pretty much immediately the big tournaments added the game to their rosters and at the first opportunity the game was included at **Evo**.

Around a year after launch the 2GGT (now known as 2GGC), events started up. These events were usually named after a prominent player, where they would fight it out against other players for the title, and there would often be some kind of bonus competition based around them. These events became very popular and nowdays are some of the biggest *Smash 4* exclusive events in the world.

The **scene** is very much dominated by North Americans, which is in part thanks to most of the major events being based in North America. However, arguably the best *Smash 4* player in the world, Gonzalo "ZeRo" Barrios, is Chilean and a new up-and-coming talent, Leonardo "MKLeo" Perez, is Mexican. Japan also has a very strong **scene** and a lot of players capable of taking the win when the two regions meet.

Compared with *Melee, Smash 4* is only just getting started, but it has already made a big mark on the esports world. Some will say that it is now the second biggest fighting game esport, behind *Street Fighter*, and it is hard to argue against that. There are some concerns, such as how long Nintendo will support a game on a now-defunct platform, but for the most part the future for *Smash 4* looks very bright.

ZERO'S INCREDIBLE RUN AT THE TOP

Gonzalo "ZeRo" Barrios is the most successful *Smash 4* player out there. He has won more big events than anyone and has made a lot of money doing so. Ever since the game first came out he has been at the very top of the **scene**, winning the big events and only rarely being beaten.

In fact ZeRo completely dominated the early days of *Smash 4* esports. From November 29, 2014 until October 26, 2015 ZeRo won every single *Smash 4* tournament he attended. This wasn't just a case of a few tournaments here or there—he had a streak of 56 competition wins during this time and was generally considered to be untouchable. During his run he lost matches here and there, but thanks to the **double elimination format** he was always able to come back and win the overall competition.

This incredible streak finally came to an end at the MLG World Finals in 2015, when Nairoby "Nairo" Quezada beat ZeRo in the playoffs. The pair had had a long love/hate rivalry going on, with Nairo coming close to beating ZeRo a few times in the playoffs. Despite this, the two were actually partners in many doubles competitions and proved just as successful. In fact the two players took the doubles competition at the MLG World Finals.

After this loss ZeRo returned to the top for a short while, but an injury brought a long run of poor form at just the wrong time and other Smashers established themselves as top contenders. He returned, and is now back as one of the best in the world, but he hasn't quite managed to get that epic winning streak back just yet.

OTHER CHALLENGERS

ELLIOT BASTIEN "ALLY" CARROZA-OYARCE

Ally had always been around the top of the **scene** during *Smash 4*, and had more than a few big wins to his name, but it wasn't until early-to mid-2016 that he really took off. With ZeRo wobbling, Ally took wins at multiple events such as GOML, and then when **Evo** rolled around he became almost unbeatable, winning the competition and establishing himself as one of the best players in the world. Since then Ally has remained at the top but has become more inconsistent than ever. He **mains** Mario, a character that many people thought was quite weak until Ally showed them how it's done.

NAIROBY "NAIRO" QUEZADA

Nairo is the player who took an event off ZeRo and, during ZeRo's run of poor form, really established himself as the best out there. He is a Zero Suit Samus **main** who always seems to find a way to win doubles competitions regardless of his partner, although the Nairo and ZeRo duo is feared by everyone. In singles competitions he constantly won events in 2015 and early 2016, but with a stronger field those big wins have become less frequent.

LEONARDO "MKLEO" PEREZ

MKLeo is the rising star of the *Smash 4* scene. At just sixteen years old the Mexican player has only recently started to compete internationally, but is already feared by most players. He hasn't been to many top-tier events, but when he is in attendance a top-four position is almost guaranteed, and anything less than top two is a disappointment. He has a long way to go, but with more events he will grow as a player, and he looks very likely to become the undisputed best player in the world.

WHO'S WHO IN GAMING

ICE FROG (DOTA 2 LEAD DESIGNER)

No one knows the real name of the lead designer of *DotA 2*. Instead, the person behind one of the biggest esports in the world goes by the name of Ice Frog, and that name has become synonymous with the game. Ice Frog was handed control of the original *DotA* mod back when the main developers went off to form Riot Games. A few years later Ice Frog was hired by **Valve** to take over *DotA 2*'s development and is credited with all the **balance changes** in the game. When a change you decide to make can impact which team takes home $10 million, you know you're a pretty important person.

GABE NEWELL (CEO OF VALVE)

Gabe Newell is a name you will know if you have ever visited a video game website in the last ten years. The CEO and founder of **Valve** is one of the most-loved people in the world of video games, and he had a big impact on esports as well. His personal contributions are limited, but he is in charge of the company that created two of the biggest esports in the world and hosts the largest esports events. He used to open The International every year, but for TI 7 he passed that responsibility on to others.

JEFF KAPLAN
(VICE PRESIDENT OF BLIZZARD/LEAD DESIGNER OF OVERWATCH)

Jeff Kaplan is another very loved name on the internet, and has become the face of *Overwatch*. Much like Ice Frog, he is credited with all of the balance decisions and changes for *Overwatch*, and is the key visionary behind the game. While it is still early on for *Overwatch*, there is no doubt that Kaplan has had a massive impact on the industry—after all his game is responsible for what could be the biggest league in esports history. A brief mention goes to Nate Nanzer, who will be the commissioner for the *Overwatch* league. Together with Kaplan he will most likely become one of the most important people in all of esports in a few years.

BRANDON "RYZE" BECK
(CEO OF RIOT GAMES)
MARC "TRYNAMERE" MERRILL
(PRESIDENT AND CMO OF RIOT GAMES)

While they may not have been the only ones to form Riot Games and work on the very first iteration of *League of Legends*, there is no doubting that this duo is one of the most important in esports. *League of Legends* is credited as a big factor in the esports boom of early 2010, and without these two there probably wouldn't be a *League of Legends*. These days they mostly work behind the scenes, keeping what is now a massive company going, but that doesn't mean they don't wield a lot of power.

WHO'S WHO IN GAMING

TEAM SOLOMID

Founded back in 2009, Team SoloMid (TSM) was originally a website for the *LoL* community, but after a while the first team was established, headed up by Andy "Reginald" Dinh. After a lot of success competitively, Reginald decided to run TSM full-time instead of playing and has grown the organization into one of the most recognizable brands in all of esports. In *LoL* TSM are the most successful NA team of all time. They are home to the most successful *Smash 4* player in the world and have had many other top teams over the years. Go to any esports event in the West and the chances are you will hear a TSM chant or two.

FNATIC

The UK-based Fnatic is a brand that is truly global, with teams in all corners of the world. They have a roster in almost every major esport, including top *DotA*, *LoL* and *CS:GO* teams. They primarily focus on team games and not individuals, and this has worked out incredibly well for them. The Fnatic fan base is one of the biggest in the world and they even have their own store in central London. Fnatic also have their own line of PC hardware and are one of the largest esports organizations in the world, with many full-time staff members.

OPTIC GAMING

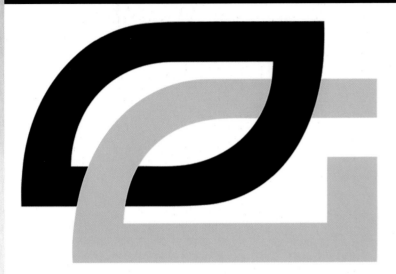

When it comes to console esports, there's no one more popular than OpTic. The organization started out in the world of *Call of Duty* and created YouTube videos, building a big following in the mid-2000s. They then fielded some pro *CoD* rosters, becoming clear fan favorites and then expanded into other titles like *Halo*, *CS:GO* and *Gears of War*.

OpTic's appeal is more than just top teams, almost every member of the organization is an internet celebrity and they all have popular YouTube channels. In recent years the organization has grown a lot, bringing in sponsorship deals from such big-name brands as Chipotle and Pepsi Co.

TEAM LIQUID

In terms of organizations that cover everything, they don't get much bigger than Team Liquid. The organization has top teams in pretty much every esport, and they even try to start up competitive scenes in games they think have potential, such as *Civilization VI*. The Liquid Organization also own the Liquipedia series of sites, which acts as a wiki for many of the top esports, while the Team Liquid website is a popular *StarCraft* forum and news site. Liquid seems to be involved with everything in the world of esports in one way or another.

THE OTHERS

There are countless esports organizations out there, and many of them can rival these four in terms of popularity or team strength. Other notable organizations include Team Dignitas, Virtus.pro, Natus, Vincere, G2 Esports, SK Gaming, FaZe Clan, Ninjas in Pyjamas, Immortals, Evil Geniuses, Splyce, Counter Logic Gaming, Team EnVyUs, Echo Fox Alliance, Invictus Gaming, LGD, and mouseports. Then of course there are sports teams such as Paris Saint-Germain and FC Schalke 04, who also have their own esports divisions.

WHO'S WHO IN GAMING

GFINITY ELITE SERIES
UK

The Gfinity Elite Series is one of the most unique events in all of esports. While most leagues are limited to one game, the Elite Series features three. The eight organizations in the competition all field teams in *Street Fighter V*, *Counter-Strike: Global Offensive* and *Rocket League*.

The competition itself is a seven-week league followed by the playoffs, where the top-four rosters in each game battle it out for a share of the $225,000 prize pool. Each Friday the *Street Fighter V* teams take to the stage, followed by the *CS:GO* players on Saturday and finally the *Rocket League* crew on Sundays. Teams play one match every week, with four matches on each day.

At the end of the playoffs, not only will the rosters that win in each competition be rewarded, but the organization that performs the best across all three games will also win the franchise championship. It's almost like the constructors championship in Formula 1.

Every week, the teams head down to the Gfinity Arena in London. The arena itself is like the set of a TV show, with a live crowd, multiple camera setups and everything you could need for a professional-looking broadcast.

While the league is just getting started, Gfinity hopes to bring the series to other areas of the world, and possibly expand it into other titles. They have already announced that the Elite Series will be coming to Australia, with more territories expected to come soon.

CHALLENGER SERIES

The Elite Series is the flashy competition that everyone wants to watch, but its sister competition, the Gfinity Challenger Series, is where some of the real magic happens. The Challenger Series is a string of online competitions that anyone can enter online. They mirror the games for the Elite Series, so (as of 2017) the Challenger Series features *SFV*, *CS:GO* and *Rocket League*.

Playing these online competitions will earn you G Points, and then at the end of each season the top players are invited to the Elite Draft. This draft of the top players is where the teams in the Elite Series sign up-and-coming talent. If signed to one of these big organizations the players will join the active roster and have the chance to play onstage for thousands of dollars.

Lots of competitions claim to make you into an esports star, but the Gfinity Elite Series is one of the only ones that has proven they can do this, and do it within a matter of weeks. If you think you can go pro then this is your best chance.

ROCKET LEAGUE

Rocket League is, at its core, very simple. The entire game is a futuristic version of soccer, where instead of humans chasing a ball and trying to put it in the goal, it's cars. A launch in mid-2015 saw *Rocket League* given to PS+ subscribers on PS4, and the game took off from there. Millions of copies were sold and the game became a megahit thanks to its simple concept but incredibly deep gameplay.

FUN FACT

Rocket League is actually a sequel to a game called *Supersonic Acrobatic Rocket-Powered Battle-Cars* that launched in 2008. You have probably never heard of it, as the game flopped, despite basically being what *Rocket League* is today. Clearly the name did not help matters . . .

A COMPETITIVE scene quickly emerged, and within a few months developers Psyonix were running a fully fledged league. The *Rocket League* Championship Series is a regular competition that offers up hundreds of thousands of dollars in prizes each season. The league has proved very popular, despite being quite young, and has already managed to bring in big sponsors such as Mobil 1, 7-Eleven, and Old Spice.

Rocket League is pretty much as simple as it sounds—cars try to knock a massive ball into a goal in the style of traditional soccer. The cars have the ability to jump, rotate in the air, boost, and climb up the walls of the arena, so there is a lot of skill involved along with some interesting tactics at the higher levels of play.

Cars playing soccer is not the most complex esport out there, but it is certainly entertaining. It features all the excitement of soccer (but at a much faster pace), and the game is played 3v3 at a competitive level, making it easy to understand. In the grand scheme of things, *Rocket League* is still a new esport, but it has the potential to challenge the biggest names out there.

ROCKET LEAGUE IS A MAINSTREAM FAVORITE

While **MOBAs** are incredibly complex and shooters are pretty violent, *Rocket League* has none of these issues that might turn off more mainstream broadcasters and events. That is why both NBC and the X Games have chosen to feature the game this year. NBC hosted a $100,000 2v2 competition in partnership with FACEIT that was broadcast on the channel and streamed online. The change in competitive format raised some eyebrows, but the massive prize pool was enough to make it a success.

The X Games, an extreme sports event that has dabbled with esports before, hosted a $75,000 invitational in Minneapolis this year. After some mediocre esports competitions at the X Games in years past, *Rocket League* provided the perfect mix between extreme sports and esports that would appeal to the X Games audience.

WORLD OF TANKS

World of Tanks is one of the most popular games in the world, mostly thanks to its success in Eastern Europe and Russia. The game boasts millions of players and is available in some form on almost every platform under the sun. As the name suggests, two teams jump into some tanks and battle it out to complete a number of objectives. The World War II setting means that this is quite a slow and tactical game, thanks to the slower-moving tanks of the time, and the incredible realism that developers Wargaming insist on. This is the closest thing to a competitive tank simulation you will ever see.

AT the competitive level, matches are played 7v7 with one team trying to attack areas of the map and the other having to defend. Rounds end when all of one team is dead, a team captures the objective, or time runs out, but for the most part it is the former that happens in pro games.

In the Western world the esports **scene** is not that popular; however in the territories where the game is popular the support is massive. CIS and Russian teams dominate the scene, with some Asian squads also doing reasonably well. At the annual world championship, known as the Grand Finals, viewing figures regularly hit the hundreds of thousands and that number does not include some broadcasts in Russia and Asia.

World of Tanks continues to grow and as a result the esports **scene** is still on the rise. It probably won't ever become as successful as some of the other major esports thanks to a lack of interest from the West, but this is an esport that will be around for years in certain territories.

NAVI  TORNADO ROX

The *World of Tanks* pro **scene** has been dominated by two teams for the last few years. NaVi and Tornado Rox, who were formerly known as Hell Raisers, have both been world champions and are always at the top end of competitors. NaVi were world champions in 2014 and 2016, while the core of the Tornado Rox team took home the wins in 2015 and 2017.

Only once have the two met in the Grand Finals of the world championship, and that was back in 2016, when it all came down to the final round. Whoever won that single round of *World of Tanks* would be world champions and take home $75,000 more than their opponents. As the round dragged on, it looked like Tornado would take the win, but in a cruel twist of fate, Yuri '"apllewOw" Lyin got stuck on a steep incline

thanks to the newly implemented realistic physics engine. He couldn't move and therefore could not get the winning kill. The remaining NaVi player picked off the other opponents and ran out the clock to claim the win in an incredibly anti-climactic moment.

This is just one example of the many great games we've seen between the two teams. You can almost guarantee that whenever they meet on **LAN**, the games will be close and most likely the best of the whole tournament. Many esports have teams that dominate the **scene**, but it feels like no one can come close to touching these two when it comes to *World of Tanks*, and their time at the top will probably last for quite a while longer yet.

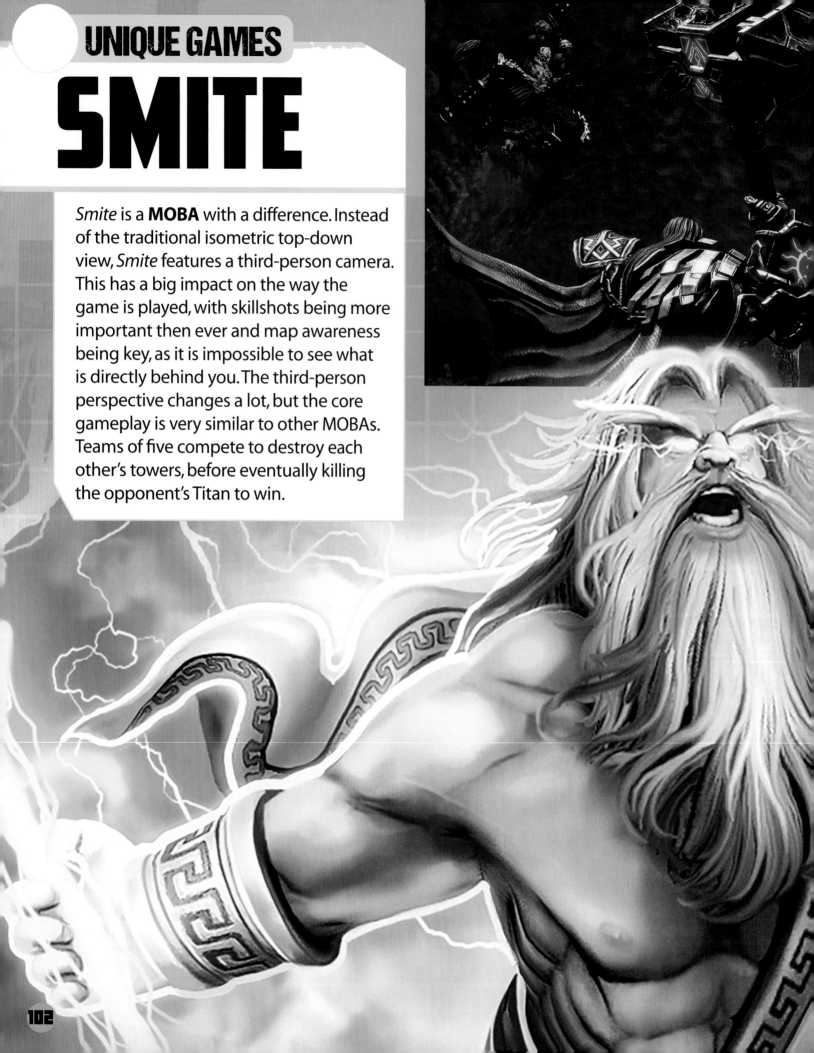

SMITE

Smite is a **MOBA** with a difference. Instead of the traditional isometric top-down view, *Smite* features a third-person camera. This has a big impact on the way the game is played, with skillshots being more important then ever and map awareness being key, as it is impossible to see what is directly behind you. The third-person perspective changes a lot, but the core gameplay is very similar to other MOBAs. Teams of five compete to destroy each other's towers, before eventually killing the opponent's Titan to win.

SMITE launched back in 2014, but had been around in alpha and beta for quite a few years prior to that. While competition was always happening within *Smite*, it wasn't really until the game officially launched that things kicked up a notch. Developers Hi Rez run pretty much everything themselves, with regular seasons and annual world championships.

Around 2015 *Smite* was close to breaking into the top tier of esports. The **scene** was boosted by a massive crowd-funding drive for its world championships, and viewing figures rocketed. Unfortunately it failed to keep this momentum and while the **scene** is still sizable, it is nowhere near as big as the other top **MOBAs**. That being said, *Smite* continues to have a solid fanbase and still has the support of a lot of big organizations, so it isn't going away anytime soon.

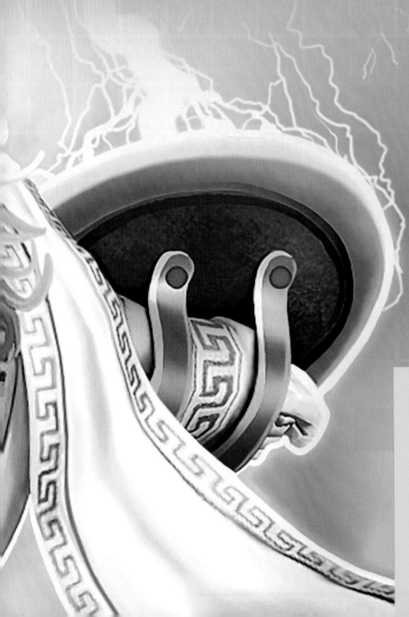

CROWD-FUNDED WORLDS

In 2014, Hi Rez announced that the prize pool for the 2015 World Championships would be crowd-funded, much like the *DotA 2* International. Some high-quality items could be purchased in-game, with some proceeds going to the prize pool. It went much better than expected and the total prize pool was a massive $2,612,259. This made it the third-biggest esports prize pool ever for a short while.

This was great for the event and brought in a lot of interest, but Hi Rez decided to cap crowd-funded prize pools for future events, to make sure that they didn't get a situation like *DotA* where they have one massive event, and the pros really only care about that. These days the prize pool is more evenly distributed across multiple events each year. However, it does show that a dedicated community can make a big difference to prize pools if given the opportunity. It also set a precedence for a lot of companies putting on similar restrictions.

GOD PASS

How heroes, or champions, are distributed in free-to-play **MOBAs** is a contentious subject. *LoL* requires you to buy each one, *HotS* has a similar model, but *DotA* gives them all away for free. Each system has its merits, but *Smite* might just have the best system of the lot! Each God can be purchased individually, but for a one-time $30 payment you can buy a pass that gives you every and any God that is released in the future.

HEARTHSTONE

Hearthstone started development with a small team at Blizzard. While the company was used to making massive titles with megabudgets and hundreds of staff, the *Hearthstone* team's mission was a little simpler. A handful of developers was given the task of coming up with a smaller-scale game in the vein of the successful indie titles that were taking the world by storm at the time. The team eventually settled on creating a card-based game and, with the *Warcraft* world at their fingertips, decided to use the established lore and characters that already existed to make it happen.

THE first iterations of *Hearthstone* were quickly made, and by all accounts the game was solid from the start. The team wanted to make sure that, despite being a digital card game, it still felt like playing a physical one. A prototype was created to show things off internally, and the game went down well. Unfortunately, the development team was then reduced in size to complete a number of other projects, before finally returning to work on *Hearthstone* some months later. However, this additional time in the schedule allowed the team to bring in a lot of new ideas to the game.

A beta started in 2013, and players instantly loved it. Beta keys became a precious commodity with almost every Blizzard fan wanting in as soon as possible. Eventually the beta opened up before the game was officially released in early 2014, and it immediately became a hit, with more people getting involved when it launched on mobile platforms. Competition was happening as early as the beta,

but once the launch happened, things really took off. Big tournament organizers such as ESL, MLG, and Gfinity put thousands of dollars into prize pools and the **scene** was quickly established. Despite originally having no plans for the game to work as an esport, Blizzard organized a world championship in 2014 and 2015 with a $250,000 prize pool, thanks to the success of third-party tournaments.

For 2016 the publisher went one step further and introduced seasonal finals that decided who made it to the world championship. These events all featured sizable prize pools of $80,000 for each region, and always featured the biggest names competing. 2016's World Championship also received a prize-pool boost, making the total prize pool $1,000,000 for the first time.

2017's competitive season followed a similar format, but this time the season events were no longer played regionally. All regions now compete at the same event for a whopping $250,000. Blizzard also introduced the *Hearthstone* Global Games, a team-based competition where players of the same nationality played with each other, similar to the *Overwatch* World Cup. This competition has a $300,000 prize pool.

Blizzard's more hands-on approach over recent years has resulted in fewer major third-party tournaments, but it has helped to keep the **scene** popular and increase prize pools across the board. Viewership is remaining pretty constant and the events continue to grow in size. So while it may be knocked out of the top tier of esports by *Overwatch* soon, it certainly isn't going anywhere.

HEARTHSTONE'S WORLD CHAMPIONS

JAMES "FIREBAT" KOSTESICH

The first-ever *Hearthstone* world champion was American player James "Firebat" Kostesich. While the World Championship was his first major-event win, he had been known as a top player for a few months, and many expected him to do quite well at the competition. After winning worlds he went on a decent streak, taking top positions at a lot of events. However, he has struggled in recent years, and these days doesn't play at many top-level **LAN** events.

SEBASTIAN "OSTKAKA" ENGWALL

In 2015, it was Sebastian "Ostkaka" Engwall who came out on top. The 2015 tournament was a huge affair, with a ton of big names making it to the event. Many of the players at the 2015 finals were popular streamers and this created massive interest in the competition. Ostkaka looked comfortable through the competition and was only pushed to his limits, when playing Thijs "Thijs" Molendijk in the semifinal. Since his win he has continued to play at some big events, but these days rarely makes it into the top four.

PAVEL "PAVEL" BELTUKOV

Pavel won the 2016 World Championship and soon established himself as the world's best, after only playing at the very top levels for around a year. He took advantage of some big names going out early, and went on to an impressive run that saw him win some very close matches. Since his win last year Pavel has remained at the top of the **scene** and continues to be one of the best in the world.

GRIM PATRON vs YOGG-SARON

In *Hearthstone*'s history many decks and cards have caused some controversy, but the two most notable at the pro level have been the Patron Warrior deck and the Yogg-Saron card. Both had very different impacts on the pro **scene**, but for a while seemed to be the only thing that people would talk about.

Grim Patron is a card that summons another Grim Patron onto the field whenever it survives a battle.

When it launched, people questioned how useful this would be. However, it was soon discovered that, if used with a Warsong Commander card, you could create an army of Patrons in one turn and win the game almost instantly. This was because the Commander card would give any minion with less than three attack the charge ability, therefore allowing it to attack on that turn.

The deck was ridiculously popular and difficult to combat, leading to almost all pros using it. Eventually the Commander was reworked and the deck died out.

Yogg-Saron has always been a strange card. When played, it will cast a random spell for every spell you have already cast in the game. So if you have cast four spells it will cast four random spells when played. This, of course, has a risk to it as spells can negatively impact the player themselves, but it can sometimes single-handedly win you a lost game.

It was initially seen as a joke card, but pros started to use it in difficult situations, and it often worked out. As it was so **RNG**-based, a lot of people said it removed the skill from the game, which Blizzard seemed to agree with, as the developers eventually nerfed the card and these days it is seen a lot less.

FORZA 6

With *Gran Turismo* being out of the limelight for some time now, it's *Forza* that has established itself as the premier racing esport. Traditionally most racing games haven't done too well as esports, especially in terms of viewer numbers. After all, the experience is very similar to that of watching real racing. There also haven't been many superstar players emerging, which is a big reason why *FIFA*, which has similar issues, has succeeded.

DESPITE the early struggles, *Forza* is slowly but surely finding its feet, and 2017 was its biggest year so far. UK event organizer Gfinity was brought in to be the official global tournament organizer for *ForzaRC*, the game's esports circuit funded by publisher Microsoft. This circuit included events taking place at Microsoft's flagship store on Fifth Avenue in New York and even at the Le Mans 24 Hours race weekend.

While *Forza* is technically an annual franchise, with a new game launching every year, it does not follow the same model as *Call of Duty* and *FIFA*, where the pro **scene** all shifts over to each new game. This is because *Forza* is split into two sub-franchises, there are the main numbered *Forza* games (that are full simulations),

and then there is *Forza Horizon* (a more arcade-style game), where players zoom around a massive open world. Interestingly *ForzaRC* supports both games, and while the primary focus is on the main *Forza* series, thanks to its simulation style, competitions are also available for *Forza Horizon*.

Going way back to the late 2000s, *Forza 2* was a part of the Championship Gaming Series, a televised esports competition that was broadcast on DirecTV and Sky. While it was only a part of the competition for a single season, more than $200,000 was given out in prize money, which at the time was a big prize pool. *Forza 2* was actually incredibly popular as an esport and arguably the most successful the franchise has ever been in the competitive environment.

FORZA RC SEASON 3: THE PORSCHE CUP AT LE MANS 24

In mid-2017, Microsoft and Gfinity hosted the finals of The Porsche Cup at Le Mans 24 Hours race. Sixty-six of the top players in the world descended on the iconic racetrack to battle it out in *Forza Motorsport 6* after winning, or placing highly, in the online competitions that preceded the event.

Unlike most racing esports, this event was a little different. Instead of being all about speed, this was also about endurance and winning the important races. Throughout the weekend the numbers were slowly whittled down, and those who made it to the final race had been playing for almost 24 hours when the event wrapped up. All that in just a couple of days.

$100,000 was up for grabs and it was Michael "AMS RoadRunner" Coyne who won the event, taking home $20,000. This was his first major-event win and it established him as one of the best *Forza* players in the world.

VAINGLORY

Vainglory was the first real mobile esport that gained any kind of traction. The game was first revealed on stage at an Apple keynote when the iPhone 6 was announced in order to show off how powerful the device was. A few months after that event, the game launched in late 2014, but things started off pretty slowly.

THE idea of a full-on **MOBA** on a mobile device was certainly a divisive one at the time. There had been many attempts to do this before, but *Vainglory* was the first title that really managed to get it right, with its unique **single lane** 3v3 format that still managed to keep all of the key **MOBA** aspects. Players started to trickle in, creating quite the active, and demanding, community, which only helped the quality of the game.

A competitive **scene** did form, with high level players competing against each other, but there was little in the way of official support for the esports side of things in the early days. Then, in 2015, Super Evil Megacorp got involved and announced some initial events, before the full seasonal competitions that dominated the first year of play.

In late 2015, the first season finals took place in Santa Ana and Katowice for NA and EU respectively, and the *Vainglory* **scene** started to pick up. Similar events throughout the following year really grew the **scene**, and big name organizations from other titles such as Team SoloMid, Team Secret and mousesports were quickly picking up *Vainglory* teams.

The first ever *Vainglory* World Championship was held in late 2016, and was another important moment for the game. For many, this was when *Vainglory* really arrived as a top esport, and with a year of top-tier events under their belts the World Championship was truly something special.

In 2017, the competitive format changed a little to become the *Vainglory Evil 8* circuit, and even more big names, such as Fnatic and Immortals, were brought into the game. Regional franchising is also being implemented, and these franchises will have the chance to host seasonal finals in their home cities. The first to do this was Fnatic with the Spring Season Unified Championships in London in early 2017.

Vainglory is expanding rapidly, and a large player base in Korea is also helping its international esports **scene**. It is easily the biggest mobile esport out there and is becoming more popular by the day.

SUPER EVIL MEGACORP

The developers and the company that runs all of the top-level esports events is called Super Evil Megacorp. However, the folks over there aren't super evil at all; in fact they are all quite lovely. Don't let the name fool you—you won't be supporting evil if you play *Vainglory*!

CLASH ROYALE

Clash Royale was one of the first games, alongside *Vainglory*, to really try to make mobile esports work. The game was developed by Supercell, the developer who also made the wildly successful *Clash of Clans* mobile game. *Clash Royale* is set in the same universe and features many of the same unit types, but is overall a very different game.

THIS 1v1 game sees both players start with a deck of cards and three towers. The map has two **lanes**, and dropping a minion card into a lane will send AI controlled characters down the lane to attack the opponent's tower. Of course your opponent will be doing the same thing so minions may fight each other before hitting towers. The first person to destroy the other king's tower, or the person with the most towers remaining after the time limit is up, is the winner.

The game is actually very simple, and can be picked up in minutes. It works well as a competitive game thanks to the deep strategy involved. The wealth of potential units to use in the game means that creating a deck of cards to take into battle is key. A poor deck can lead to an almost instant loss in some cases, and at the top end a **meta** is very much established to decide the top cards.

Then there is the trying to outsmart your opponent factor. If you can trick them into unleashing their entire army, for you to swiftly kill them and launch a devastating counterattack, then things are looking good. The three-minute game time means that matches are fast-paced and players have to think incredibly quickly, but also plan their moves well ahead of time.

Clash Royale has a lot of things that work in its favor, such as its easy free-to-play model, the ability to play anywhere, and its surprising depth. Mobile esports are still a very young industry, but games like *Clash Royale* and *Vainglory* are proving that they can, and do, work.

COKE ESPORTS

When *Clash Royale* first launched, early competitions started to do incredible numbers. Small events that were quickly put together were bringing in hundreds of thousands of viewers and top streamers were fighting against the big names in *LoL* and *CS* for viewers. This, of course, attracted a lot of sponsors, and probably the most notable major supporter of *Clash Royale* is Coke esports.

The esports arm of Coca-Cola was set up a few years back, but mainly took a back-seat role, sponsoring a few events here and there and organizing viewing parties in movie theaters for the major tournaments of the year. Nowadays, Coke esports runs its own *Clash Royale* tournaments most weeks and is heavily involved in the **scene**. It is one of the biggest sponsors of the game, and its involvement has boosted the **scene** significantly.

THE CROWN CHAMPIONSHIP

The first ever Crown Championship was a million-dollar tournament that let up to a million players enter through the game itself. This massive competition then whittled down the players until the very best headed to London to compete for the lion's share of the impressive prize pool. Who says mobile esports can't be big?

WORLD RECORDS

HIGHEST-EARNING FEMALE PRO PLAYER

It's no secret that the world of esports is dominated by men. Almost all of the biggest teams in the world are made up of male players. However, there is a strong core of female players in every game, and many of them have done quite well for themselves.

The most successful female player of all time is Sasha "Scarlett" Hostyn, who has won over $188,000 playing *StarCraft II*. She is one of the only Western players, regardless of gender, who can challenge the big Korean names, and as a result has become one of the best players in the world. Perhaps the bigger achievement is that she also inspired many other female players to try to enter the world of esports.

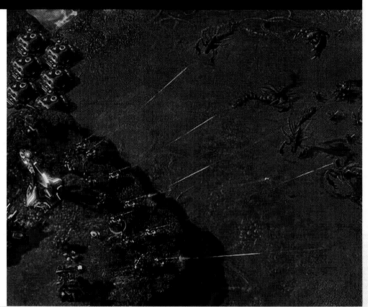

YOUNGEST-EVER PROFESSIONAL GAMER

According to Guinness World Records, the youngest-ever pro gamer is Victor "Lil Poison" De Leon III. He entered his first tournament at age four, competing in the MLG *Halo* circuit of events. By the time he was seven he had a pro contract with MLG competing on the *Halo* circuit, becoming the youngest pro gamer ever.

In 2007, he proved that this hype was totally deserved as he placed second in the largest *Halo 2* freefall event ever. More than 500 people had signed up for the competition, and Lil Poison only fell in the final match.

THE FIRST GAME TO GIVE AWAY OVER $100,000,000 IN PRIZE MONEY

It probably isn't that surprising that *DotA 2* was the first game to hit this milestone. After all, The International has given away more than $40 million over just the last two years, but if you go back just five years this figure would have been near unthinkable.

It has only been the last few years where the prize pool of The International has hit truly ridiculous levels. The first two competitions featured $1.6 million, which these days is about average for a world championship, and even the first crowd-funded International, TI 3, didn't break the $3 million mark. It was from TI 4 onwards where things go really big, and the amount of money given away started to pull way ahead of other titles.

The $100,000,000 mark was broken before the prize pool for The International 7 was added to the total, and well before the new Major system contributed anything to it. When this massive figure was broken, more than 50 percent of the total prize pool had been given away at The International; with the TI 7 prize pool added on that percentage will have only increased.

This shows just how heavily weighted the *DotA* scene is towards The International, and explains why **Valve** wanted to introduce more major tournaments for the upcoming season.

To put this impressive record into perspective, the next-closest game in terms of prize money is *League of Legends*, with a total of $41,890,164.13, and just behind that is *CS:GO*, with $37,386,103.05. Both still have a long way to go to catch up to *DotA* though…

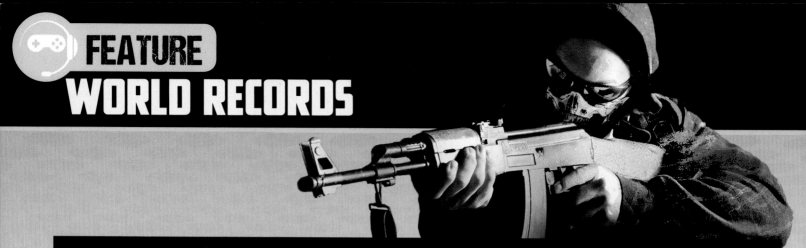

MOST CONCURRENT VIEWERS ON A SINGLE TWITCH STREAM

While events have been bringing in millions of viewers for years, they have always been split across multiple broadcasts which distort the true numbers. However, for the first time ever, in 2017, a single **Twitch** stream broke the one-million-concurrent-viewers mark.

The final for the ELEAGUE *CS:GO* Major managed to break one million concurrent viewers on the English-language **Twitch** stream. This was the first time this happened on **Twitch**, and showed just how popular that tournament was.

Over 1,026,000 people tuned in to watch the final of the competition that saw Astralis take home their first world championship, defeating the Polish side Virtus.pro in one of the closest finals seen in the world of *CS:GO*.

There were many reasons why this final proved to be so popular. The stellar event production and quality of the Major had drawn in a lot of viewers, while many viewers tuned in to watch the two best teams in the world battle it out for supremacy. Then, of course, there was the fact that this was held in a time zone where many regions could watch at a time that didn't involve being awake past midnight, and that it didn't clash with any other major events. All of this resulted in a great broadcast that deservedly ended up breaking records.

BIGGEST ESPORTS LAN EVENT

According to figures released by ESL, the biggest esports **LAN** event of all time was the 2017 iteration of the Intel Extreme Masters Katowice competition. IEM Katowice serves as the big end-of-season event for the Intel Extreme Masters, and in 2017 that competition featured *League of Legends, CS:GO* and *StarCraft II*.

The event was held at the Spodek Arena in the Polish town of Katowice, and brought in 173,000 fans over the course of the event which spanned two weekends. These fans came to watch the top *League of Legends* teams in the first weekend, and then the top *CS:GO* and *StarCraft* players on the second weekend. The second weekend also featured a much larger expo that included *Heroes of the Storm* competitions, and many other sponsor booths and activities to take part in.

The event was also a massive success online, with over 46 million unique viewers tuning in to watch the competition at different stages over the two weekends.

$650,000 was up for grabs across the three titles, and the action was fierce. Astalis won the *CS:GO* competition, Flash Wolves won the *LoL* competition and Jun "TY" Taw Yang won the *StarCraft* competition.

Things don't get much bigger than IEM Katowice in terms of esports, and it is certainly worth attending if you ever get the chance.

FEATURE

THE WORLD OF ESPORTS

Legendary *DotA 2* player and former world champion Danil "Dendi" Ishutin studies his notes before a crucial game at ESL One Frankfurt 2016. While *DotA* is a game that relies on quick decision-making, the pre-game draft, where players select the heroes they will play, requires a lot of strategy and pre-planned ideas. Some players have been known to take documents larger than this book onto the stage to cover all the possibilities.

The fans are what keep the world of esports going, and the passion they show at every event is amazing! Here a Team Liquid fan shows his support mid-game, despite being in an area full of opposing fans. While rivalries between teams can be heated, all of the fans love each other and there is never any bad blood between supporters.

THE WORLD OF ESPORTS

The equipment a pro gamer chooses is vital to their success. They need the most-reliable accessories that allow them to play at their best. In the console world companies such as Scuf create controllers that are designed to help the very top players, making things more comfortable for long-term play and adding extra functionality.

OpTic Gaming's *CoD* team celebrates a crucial round win. For these players there is more than just money on the line—this is their chance to be the very best at what they do, on an international stage. Very few people can ever claim to be the best in the world, especially in something as popular as *Call of Duty*. Ask any player why they compete and the answer will always be because they want to be a true world champion!

The Intel Extreme Masters Katowice event is one of the biggest esports events in the world, with tens of thousands of people attending. While this is an example of one of the larger events, there are many others of a similar size. In fact there probably isn't a month that goes by where there isn't a massive stadium event in the world of esports. This isn't just a few people playing for inflated amounts of money—this is truly a massive worldwide activity that millions of people enjoy!

It's one thing to watch your favorite esports players slug it out in online matches, but for many fans there's nothing quite like the thrill of attending an event in person. At the packed Epicenter in Saint Petersburg, Russia, hardcore *Counter-Strike: Global Offensive* fans get to rub shoulders with fellow like-minded gamers. Being part of an incredible live event like this is what has elevated esports to the worldwide phenomenon it is today.

GLOSSARY

BALANCE CHANGES

Competitive games will often receive software patches that change certain things in the game. This is referred to as a balance change, as the developers are trying to make everything as fair as possible, so one character or strategy is not too strong.

BATTLE.NET

Blizzard's app for buying, downloading and launching all Blizzard games. Battle.net is also credited as the software behind the matchmaking in Blizzard games.

CASTER

A caster, or shout caster, is the person (or persons) that commentates on esports games.

CLOUD SAVING

The ability to store your saved game file in the Cloud, allowing you to access it from any compatible device simply by signing in. This means you don't actually have to manually transfer saved game files.

COVER-BASED

A mechanic in a game that allows characters to take cover and hide behind an object.

DLC

Abbreviation for Downloadable Content. This can be extra content or features, usually released once a game has been launched, that players can download at a cost or for free.

DOUBLE ELIMINATION FORMAT

This type of competition bracket means that those in the winners or upper side of the bracket can lose one game and then go into the lower bracket. If they lose the lower bracket, they are out of the competition. One person or team will make it to the final from the winners bracket, and the other from the losers bracket.

EVO

Evo is short for the Evolution tournament, which is the biggest fighting-game tournament in the world.

FGC

An abbreviation for Fighting Game Community. The FGC is the all-encompassing term for anything to do with fighting-game esports, and is commonly used to describe the fans of the games.

FIFA ULTIMATE TEAM GAME MODE

A game mode within *FIFA* where players open packs of digital cards to try and form a team of players, and then use that team to play games online. There is also a marketplace where cards can be bought and sold for in-game currency.

FPS

An abbreviation for First-Person Shooter, a genre of video game that includes games such as *Call of Duty*, *Counter Strike: Global Offensive* and *Halo*.

GRASSROOTS SCENES

Low-level local competition and tournaments. The grassroots scene is used to describe many of the smaller tournaments that get little attention but allow anyone and everyone to join in.

IGL

Abbreviation for In-Game Leader. The IGL is kind of like the team captain, and will be the one who calls the strategies and tactics in-game. They will be the tactical mastermind and the other players will listen to them.

LAN

Abbreviation for Local Area Network, a computing term where PCs are connected together directly instead of using the internet. In esports it is used to describe an event where players will be playing in the same location. It comes from the computers being connected by LAN.

MAIN

Referring to the main character a person will play as. For instance, if someone is a Fox Main, that means their preferred character is Fox.

META

The use of meta changes from game to game, but it generally describes the strategies that are considered to be the best by the pro players. The meta will change quite often in most games.

MID LANER

The player who plays in the mid lane in a MOBA. This is considered by many to be the star role, as they will mostly play 1v1 against the other mid laner.

MOBA

An abbreviation for Multiplayer Online Battle Arena. This is a genre of video game that houses games such as *DotA 2*, *League of Legends*, *Heroes of the Storm* and many more.

PICKUP GROUP LEAGUES

Online competitions where you join with other random online players to form a team. These teams are called Pickup Groups or PuGs.

PVP

An abbreviation for Player vs Player games. This is where two or more real-life people play against each other.

RNG

Abbreviation for Random Number Generation. RNG is used to describe chance or luck, when something has a random outcome. For instance, if you need to roll higher than 98 to win, and you roll 99, that is positive RNG.

SCENE

The word used to describe all areas of an esport, including the tournaments, community, and anything else related to the game being played competitively.

SINGLE LANE

A term used to describe *Vainglory's* map. Most MOBAs will feature three lanes, but *Vainglory* only features one.

SPECTATOR MODE

A built-in set of tools that allows a person to view competitive matches within a game itself. A good spectator mode will feature things such as a controllable camera and the ability to highlight certain items.

SPLIT

Usually two splits (spring and summer), each consist of eight teams playing one another over a period of approximately ten weeks.

STRAT

Short for strategy.

TWITCH

The broadcast platform that most esports broadcasts can be found on.

VALVE

An entertainment software and technology company that has created some of the world's leading games and developed leading-edge technology.

WEATHERMAN SEGMENTS

A portion of a broadcast where a presenter will analyze what happened in a match on a screen behind them, almost looking like someone presenting a weather forecast.

XFL-STYLE FAILURE

The XFL was an American football league created by WWE owner Vince McMahon. The league flopped and is credited as one of the biggest high-profile failures in sports, only running for one season.

ISBN 978-0-06-289414-4

18 19 20 21 22 23 PC/LSCW 10 9 8 7 6 5 4 3 2 1

❖

First Edition
Originally published in the UK by Studio Press, an imprint of Kings Road Publishing.

Picture credits:
itlada/Shutterstock.com: p6–13, 34–39, 54–59, 68-77, 92-95, 114–117, 126-128
adamziaja.com/Shutterstock.com: p122–123;
Volodymyr Goinyk/Shutterstock.com: p69; F8 studio/Shutterstock.com: p69;
Romankosolapov/Shutterstock.com:p124-125
Photo: Facebook: p69
Tech Luimnal: p92

All other images: Joe Brady

Thanks to:
Gfinity
ESL
The Coalition
Turtle Beach